ALSO BY TOM BROKAW
AVAILABLE FROM RANDOM HOUSE
LARGE PRINT

An Album of Memories

The Greatest Generation Speaks

The Greatest Generation

A LONG WAY FROM HOME

TOM BROKAW

A LONG WAY FROM HOME

Growing Up in
the American Heartland

RANDOM HOUSE
LARGE PRINT

Library of Congress Cataloging-in-Publication Data
Brokaw, Tom.
A long way from home/ Tom Brokaw.
p. cm.
ISBN 0-375-43185-3
1. Brokaw, Tom.   2. Television news anchors—
United States—Biography.   3. Television journalists—
United States—Biography.   4. National characteristics,
American.   5. Large type books.   I. Title.

PN4874.B717 A3 2002
070'.92—dc21
[B] 2002075166

www.randomlargeprint.com

FIRST LARGE PRINT EDITION

10 9 8 7 6 5 4 3 2 1

This Large Print edition published in accord
with the standards of the N.A.V.H.

For Mother

Acknowledgments

Over the years, as I've shared stories of my South Dakota boyhood and family history, friends have often said, "When are you going to write that in a book?," an idea I have successfully resisted until now. I worried that such a book could be seen as simply an exercise in vanity, rather than as what I hoped it would be, an attempt to document the manner in which I was raised in the America of the post–World War II years. I wanted to get beyond an anchorman's inflated sense of self-importance (an oxymoron?) and express my gratitude to the people who raised me, and to the character of life in the American heartland from which I have drawn so much. In any case, this is a book about my life until the age of twenty-two, when I left South Dakota.

One of the perils of embarking on such a book is that the prism through which you look back on your own life gives off a certain rosy tint. I have tried to avoid that, but it is also true that I grew up as a congenital optimist at a time when everything seemed possible in America, especially for a white male, and among people accustomed to difficult challenges, hard work, and productive results. I am also aware that I happened to be born in the right place at the right time, and to the right set of parents, who did not limit my dreams of a different kind of life.

I am deeply grateful for the assistance I've received along the way, especially from my family, beginning with my mother, Jean Brokaw, and my wife, Meredith. They have been, as always, insightful and sensible in their comments and encouragement. Meredith and my daughters, Jennifer, Andrea and Sarah, provided invaluable observations as well.

I am also extremely grateful for the long and detailed history of the Brokaw family provided by the genealogists at the headquarters of the Church of Jesus Christ of Latter-day Saints in Salt Lake City. It is a true treasure for our family.

Sarah Hodder and Phil Napoli were tireless and resourceful in their pursuit of the factual history of the Great Plains, the small towns where I lived and the time about which I wrote. Sarah, particularly, became an expert on turn-of-the-century development in northern South Dakota, dam construction on the Missouri River, and the social and political evolution of my hometown.

At NBC, I could always count on the energetic, efficient, and good-humored assistance of Sara Perkowski and Meaghan Rady. They have been peerless in their ability to organize and manage the NBC News part of my life when I was in a time-consuming phase of the book.

At Random House, Benjamin Dreyer, Richard Elman, Jolanta Benal, and Frankie Jones were indispensable and patient as they helped convert the manuscript into book form. Thank you all.

Carole Lowenstein and Daniel Rembert deserve special thanks for framing my words with photos and mementos going back a century.

What can I say about Kate Medina, my editor at Random House? This is our fourth book together, and there would have been none without her. In her cool, elegant way she gives me the courage to start and the advice that makes it possible to keep going. Kate plants good ideas and uproots bad ones, constantly tending the landscape of our common turf, always nudging me to higher ground.

Her assistant, Jessica Kirshner, was the master of logistics and the calm, friendly stalwart who deftly handled all of the incoming calls, photos, queries, and manuscripts. Whatever else happens in the world, Jessica, we'll always have our e-mail.

When I was in the final stages of my first book, *The Greatest Generation,* I asked two friends, Kurt Andersen and Frank Gannon, to read it. They were so generous with their time and so astute in their observations that I've taken advantage of them again. Their comments on content, style, and theme were immeasurably helpful. Thank you, gentlemen.

Having said that, whatever mistakes, slights, oversights, and overstatements are contained herein, I am responsible. Because of the particular nature of this book, I did rely a great deal on personal memory, and although I pride myself on recall, I know that others may remember events in other ways.

I greatly regret that I couldn't mention by name everyone who was important to me as I was growing up. There were so many people—

from pals, girlfriends, and role models to teachers and friends of my parents. I am indebted to you all.

When I sent this book to my mother for her comments and corrections, she wrote back to say, "In some parts your ego is showing, but mostly it's fine." Forty years after I left home for the last time, she still has my number.

Contents

Contents

A LONG WAY FROM HOME

CHAPTER I

A Long Way from Home

IN 1962, I PUT MY HOME STATE OF SOUTH Dakota in a rearview mirror and drove away. I was uncertain of my final destination but determined to get well beyond the slow rhythms of life in the small towns and rural culture of the Great Plains. I thought that the influences of the people, the land, and the time during my first twenty-two years of life were part of the past. But gradually I came to know how much they meant to my future, and so I have returned often as part of a long pilgrimage of renewal.

When I do return, my wardrobe and home address are New York, my job is high-profile, and my bank account is secure, but when I enter a South Dakota café or stop for gas, I am

Dad and me during the summer of 1943.

just someone who grew up around here, left a while back, and never really answers when he's asked, "When you gonna move back home?" I am caught in that place all too familiar to small-state natives who have moved on to a rewarding life in larger arenas: I don't want to move back, but in a way I never want to leave. I am nourished by every visit.

On those trips back to the Great Plains I always try to imagine the land before it was touched by rails and plows, fences and roads. I can still drive off the pavement of South Dakota highways, find a slight elevation in the prairie flatness, and look to a distant horizon, across untilled grassland, and with no barbed wire or telephone poles or dwellings to break the plane of earth and sky. It is at once majestic and intimidating. More than a century after the first white settlers began to arrive, the old Dakota Territory remains a place where nature rules.

On a still, hot late-summer day, after a wet spring in the northern plains of South Dakota, the rich golden fields of wheat and barley, the deep green landscapes of corn and alfalfa surrounding the neat white farmhouses framed by red barns and rows of sheltering trees, give a

*My mother, Jean Conley,
declared the healthiest girl in Day
County, South Dakota, 1930.*

glow of goodness and prosperity. It is hard to remember this was once a place of despair brought on by a cruel combination of nature and economic forces at their most terrifying.

This was a bleak and hostile land in the Dirty Thirties.

Families struggled against drought, grasshoppers, collapsed markets, and fear. Billowing clouds of topsoil, lifted off the land by fierce winds, reduced the sun to a faint orb; in April 1934, traces of Great Plains soil were found as far east as Washington, D.C. One report said the dust storm was so bad it left a film on President Franklin D. Roosevelt's Oval Office desk.

This is where my mother and father were raised and came of age, at the height of the Depression. It is where I was born and spent the first twenty-two years of my life, and it remains always familiar, however long I have been away. Whenever I return, I try to imagine the struggles my parents and everyone else went through here in the thirties. That time formed them—and through them, it formed me. I am in awe of how they emerged, and I am grateful for their legacy, although I have been an imperfect steward.

When I left in 1962, I was hungry for bright

I'm at the wheel of my Uncle Lloyd's tractor, in 1946.

Mother and Dad, my brothers, Bill and Mike, and me (on the far right), on a visit to Bristol in the forties

lights, big cities, big ideas, and exotic places well beyond the conventions and constraints of my small-town childhood, but forty years later I still call South Dakota home. Time and distance have sharpened my understanding of the forces that shaped my parents' lives and mine so enduringly. Those forces are the grid on which I've come to rely, in good times and bad.

In the late 1800s, the Dakota Territory was one of the last frontiers in America, a broad, flat grassland where Sitting Bull, Crazy Horse, and their followers in the Sioux nation were hunters and warriors on horseback, determined to hold their land against the persistent invasion of white settlers who wanted to farm, ranch, and build towns along the railroad lines racing westward from the industrialized East and Midwest.

The Sioux won some battles, notably Little Big Horn in Montana, but they lost the war. The Dakota Territory was divided into two states, one north and one south, in 1889. My ancestors were among the early settlers in what became South Dakota.

My father, Anthony Orville Brokaw, was born on October 17, 1912, the last of ten children of William and Elizabeth Brokaw. His

The Brokaw House,
the family-run hotel in Bristol—
one of my early homes.

grandfather Richard P. Brokaw, the descendant of Huguenots who immigrated early to New York, had made his way to the southwestern Dakota Territory by covered wagon following the Civil War. He farmed and worked on the railroad before heading north in 1881 to found the town of Bristol and a small hotel, the Brokaw House, at the planned intersection of the north-south and east-west rail lines, eight years before statehood.

My mother is the eldest daughter of Jim and Ethel Conley, who farmed south of Bristol. Ethel took the train from Bristol to Minneapolis, her hometown, for Jean's birth; then mother and daughter returned to the remote corner of the prairie where Jim was tilling the ground behind teams of horses.

In the summer of 1996 my mother and I returned to the northern plains, the womb of her life and mine, for a visit that was at once nostalgic, reassuring, and a commentary on the social and economic changes in this country in the second half of the twentieth century.

As we drove east along Highway 12 from Aberdeen, South Dakota, toward Bristol, we passed a giant Wal-Mart with a parking lot full of late-model cars and pickup trucks; there were expensive new houses on large lots, and broad streets well beyond the city limits; giant John Deere combines, worth more than $100,000 apiece, moved efficiently through ripe fields of wheat, disgorging the small, valuable kernels into a truck of the kind called a Twin Hopper for its side-by-side bins that can hold a combined total of one thousand bushels. Many of the combines have air-conditioning and stereos in their cabs, to go with the computer monitoring systems that record the yield while the harvest is under way. Many of the smaller farms have been consolidated into larger tracts and organized as corporations with sophisticated business models relying on the efficiencies of mass production and the yield of genetically engineered grains. Much has changed, but still, a drought or a sudden hailstorm or a freak cold snap can undo all of the best planning and agriculture science.

Modern technology hasn't completely eliminated what my mother remembers of the sweat and heartache required for a farmer's life. But it is a far different world than when I was a child. As a town kid, I was attracted to the farm only by the prospect of a horseback ride or the chance to drive a tractor. I had no inclination for the work, much of it unending and involving uncooperative livestock in a muck of mud and manure or working in fields beneath a blazing sun.

South Dakota is two states, really, divided by the Missouri River. In a larger sense, the river also divides the Midwest from the West. East of the Missouri, in the midwestern half, small towns shaded by trees planted a hundred years ago are separated by clusters of farm buildings and quadrangles of tilled ground producing corn, soybeans, wheat, rye, and sunflowers.

As you move across the Missouri, into what we call West River country, the change is abrupt. On airplanes flying across South Dakota east to west, I like to tell my fellow passengers to watch the cultivated fields, the gold and green color schemes of corn and wheat, suddenly give way to the muted browns and the untilled sod once we cross the river. It is such a stunning change, it is as if someone flipped a page, and then another change comes two hundred miles farther. At the very western edge of the state, the prairie breaks up into the arid and eerily beautiful Badlands and then gives way to the Black Hills, a small scenic mountain range the Sioux people called Paha Sapa, the most sacred of their land.

I have lived and traveled in every quarter of

the state, and I am constantly struck by the rawness of it all, even now, more than 125 years after the first significant wave of white settlers began trying to tame it. A summer night can be a reminder of the primal forces of the old Dakota Territory when a storm blows up, filling the sky with mountainous thunderstorms and bowing the tall cottonwoods with cold winds that seem to begin somewhere near the Arctic Circle.

I am particularly attached to the Missouri River, that ancient artery that begins in central Montana and powers its way north before beginning its long east-by-southeast trek across the flat landscape of the Dakotas and along the borders of Iowa, Nebraska, and Missouri. Large dams have slowed but not completely conquered the river of Lewis and Clark, the Sioux, Crow, Omaha, and Santee tribes. Whenever I return to my home state I always try to swim in the river channel, just to feel its restless currents again, as a reminder of my early struggles to master them as a beginning swimmer. They taught me to understand force and use it to my advantage, taught me that to make progress often means giving a little.

On this trip back to Bristol with my mother

in 1996, as I steered our rental car toward the distant eastern horizon, an old sensation returned. Up there in the northern latitudes, less than two hundred miles from the Canadian border, I feel as if I am riding the curvature of the earth, silhouetted against the sweeping arc of sky that so diminishes all below. I have now lived two thirds of my life outside these familiar surroundings, yet whenever I return I am at peace, and always a little excited to know that this place has a claim on me.

I am named for my maternal great-grandfather Thomas Conley, the son of Irish immigrants, who was working as a railroad conductor in St. Paul when he was attracted by the abundance of affordable farmland in Day County, South Dakota. Tom and his wife, Mathilda, moved in 1897 to Webster, the Day County seat, where Tom opened a saloon before moving on to a section and a half of prairie, 960 acres, southwest of Bristol, where together he and Mathilda began farming with horse-drawn machinery.

Tom Conley, at six feet a tall man in those days, quickly established a reputation as a hard-working and efficient farmer who, according to local lore, took off only one day a year: the

Fourth of July. On Independence Day he'd drive a horse-drawn wagon from the farm to Bristol's main street for the celebrations, shouting to everyone, "Hurray for the Fourth of July!"

Tom and Mathilda Conley prospered in the early days of the twentieth century, sending three of their four sons to college. One went on to law school and another to medical school. My mother's father, Jim, graduated from a pharmacy college in Minneapolis, but he preferred farming to pharmacy and returned to Day County with his bride, Ethel Baker, a handsome and lively daughter of a foreman at Pillsbury Mills in the Twin Cities. As a wedding present, Tom Conley gave his son and new wife as a wedding present a mortgaged quarter-section, 160 treeless acres just north of his farm. It was so barren that Jim Conley often said it contained not even a rusty nail; black-and-white pictures from that time are startling in their bleakness.

A quarter-section of land was the allotment that the seminal figure of prairie literature, Per Hansa, filed for when he took his family into the Dakota Territory, in O. E. Rolvaag's classic *Giants in the Earth*. Powerful winds, broad horizons, "And sun! And still more sun!"—as

Rolvaag vividly described this part of America that stretches from the Canadian border to Oklahoma, from Minnesota to the middle of Montana.

It was little changed in the first quarter of the twentieth century, when my parents were youngsters. Just as for Per Hansa and his fellow Norwegian settlers, it was a demanding place, whatever the season, for those who came to farm or to establish the small towns where agriculture and commerce intersected across the grassland. It is a place that reflects a century of transformation in America.

When my mother was born, in November 1917, the world was in turmoil. That same month Lenin took control of the Russian government and the Communist revolution was under way. America entered World War I at last, and General John Pershing led American forces into Europe. The war was an international tragedy but a bonanza for American farmers, as they moved into mechanized equipment and turned their grain fields into the bread basket of the world. Farmland in the heart of the corn belt brought prices two and three times what they had been just three years earlier.

Jim and Ethel were making enough money

to start a new home and buy a Model T, the little black car that was the centerpiece of Henry Ford's rapidly growing empire. Neither of my grandparents left behind a personal account of their hopes and dreams, but I suspect they thought the farm would become their life work. Instead, it became a heartbreaking burden.

By 1930 they were trapped between a prolonged drought across the Great Plains and economic chaos in the international markets. Jim and Ethel, my mother, Jean, and her younger sister, Marcia, were hostage to the cruelties of what came to be known as the Great Depression. Between 1929 and 1932, the average net per capita income on family farms fell from $2,297 to $74.

Jim Conley admired Herbert Hoover, a native of nearby Iowa and a brilliant mining engineer who was an international hero for his organization of food programs for Europe following the devastation of World War I. It is likely that Jim voted for Hoover in the 1928 presidential election. But what happened in the thirties would make my grandfather an ardent Democrat for his remaining days.

Jim and Ethel Conley's hopes for a long life

on the farm were wiped out. By 1932, Jim was feeding his corn crop to his hogs because doing so was more economical than taking it to market, where it would have brought less than a nickel a bushel. By my mother's junior year in high school, the Conley farm days were over. The bank foreclosed and the family moved to nearby Bristol.

Because my parents came of age during the Great Depression, it never completely left their consciousness. It would be too melodramatic to say they carried lasting scars, but it would be equally inaccurate to describe the Depression as just a benign passage in their lives. The residual effect went well beyond the bleak economics of the time. Living through the Great Depression formed other lasting values: an uncompromising work ethic, thrift, compassion, and, perhaps most important, perspective.

My parents and their friends were members of the "waste not, want not" generation. They measured everything from food to wrapping paper to soap for its potential secondary value. No scrap of food was summarily disposed of without first getting an evaluation from Mother on its leftover possibilities. Sunday's leftover mashed potatoes became Monday night's fried potato patties. Gifts were opened carefully, and the wrapping paper was folded and put away for another gift later on. When bars of soap became so small they hardly seemed worth saving, they were pressed onto other bars in the same condition. Worn-out T-shirts became dust rags. Nails pulled out of boards were hammered back into shape and stored in an empty coffee can. A friend's father could never get used to the idea of paper towels. He used them carefully and dried them for another time.

Sometime after I left South Dakota, I returned and hosted a cocktail party for home-state friends at my hotel. I gave Dad a fistful of cash and asked him to buy several bottles of expensive name-brand liquor. He returned with most of the money still in hand and a collection of cheap generic booze. When I protested he said, "Why waste your money on that expensive stuff? After the first drink, they don't know the difference anyway."

Theirs was a generation whose members were so conditioned by the economic perils of their upbringing that they sometimes carried caution and frugality to a fault. At a stage in their lives when they could easily afford personal indulgences, they were still reluctant to spend money on anything that wasn't practical. For a long time they refused to believe that the Great Depression was a once-in-a-lifetime event.

While we joke in our family that I have somehow managed to adapt to other economic conditions, I still have a visceral reaction to waste or excess. I never fail to wonder, "Is this really necessary?" I continue to look at price tags first, and nothing pleases me more than a great bargain, just as few things distress me more than a foolish purchase.

My father, who was known as Red most of his life because of his flaming hair, died in 1982, too young at age sixty-nine, but he had accomplished far more than he could have imagined in the early, difficult days of his childhood. Mother, five years younger than my father, is alive and flourishing, a resident of Southern California, where she has an active social life of travel, plays, and bridge club, personal-computer time and great-grandmother duties. She's a model matriarch for three generations of children and grandchildren.

Her wardrobe has changed from midwestern sensible to California panache. She watches the Dodgers and the Lakers on television. As she always did, she follows the news closely, except now she has reason to call one of the newscasters personally when she disagrees with something he said or dislikes a tie he wore that day.

My brother Bill, next in line in our family, lives in Denver, where he's involved in real estate after a long career managing restaurants. Mike, the youngest of the Brokaw boys, and a knockoff of Red, is a foreman for a Southern California telephone company. So we're scattered now, but our heritage remains out there in the small towns and grassy plains of America's own savannah, a great stretch of landscape that retains many of its nineteenth-century qualities.

In 1972, I returned to South Dakota on assignment for NBC News from my home in Los Angeles. I drove through the center of the state on a cloudy autumn night when there were no stars or moon visible for illumination. I stopped the car on a desolate stretch of highway to take it all in, and when I stepped into the void, I was momentarily unsettled by the overwhelming sense of isolation. Then I laughed aloud, remembering that I drove fearlessly through the toughest neighborhoods in Southern California and on the crowded and dangerous freeways of that state.

When Mother and I returned in 1996, she was alternately chatty and pensive at my side, realizing that there might not be many more trips to the small towns and countryside that she had called home. It was a kind of spiritual pilgrimage, as we made the turnoff that would take us to the farm where she had lived until she was sixteen. She leaned forward on the passenger side, looking for landmarks, momentarily confused by her memory of a treeless plain and narrow dirt roads where now there were mature cottonwoods and a two-lane paved highway.

Then, there it was: the Conley farm. Once it had been a collection of primitive buildings and a small unpainted house perched atop a grassy prairie; now it was a prosperous-looking ensemble of a white two-story house, a red barn, and a granary tucked into a thick grove of trees. A few miles away, her grandfather Tom's farm had disappeared. All that remained were a few old trees from the grove he had planted.

As we drove down the country lanes, Mother ticked off the names of the families who had once settled here on their own 160-acre plots, now long abandoned to the efficiencies of much larger corporate farms. Her neighbors were mostly of Scandinavian and German descent, the dominant ethnic groups in South Dakota, drawn by the same lure as her father: cheap land and an independent life, a claim on the promise of the prairie as a reliable producer of grain and a friendly environment for livestock.

The effect of the consolidation of agriculture and the demise of railroading could be seen in the diminished prospects of Bristol, a few miles north of the farm. Bristol reached its peak population of 675 in 1940. Until then it had grown modestly but steadily as a trade center for local farmers and travelers on the Milwaukee Railroad and on U.S. Highway 12, a main east-west artery in the days before the interstate. Bristol had two new car dealerships, two banks, two hotels, four cafés, a creamery, a newspaper, a movie theater, farm implement dealers and grain dealers, and a doctor. Now Bristol's population is less than 400, but the town hasn't given up: a young couple has established on Main Street a mail-order company selling made-in-Dakota products. Others have banded together to form a grocery cooperative so they don't have to drive to Webster, the county seat, twelve miles away, for necessities. There are two seed companies, a grain elevator, a bowling alley, and a service station operated by the Farmers Union, a cooperative.

The Brokaw House, the three-story hotel established by my great-grandfather, anchored Main Street's north end until it was torn down in 1962. A few of my parents' nieces and nephews and their childhood friends remain in the area, but the Brokaw and Conley names now are prominent mainly on the headstones in the family plots at the Bristol and Webster cemeteries.

As I watched my mother absorb all the changes in the landscape of her childhood and contemplate the development of her life from that time and place to the present, I was again reminded of how I have benefited from being a close witness to her steady-as-she-goes attitude, the rewards of a focused, temperate approach to whatever challenges arose. She embodies the pragmatism and utilitarianism of the culture in which she was raised, and of her life with Red.

When my wife's parents and Mother's sister all died within a short period, Mother was suddenly the sole surviving senior member of several families. She became a matriarch, and grandmother to nephews and nieces as well as to her own grandchildren. It was a role she simply assumed, and it was a continuation of her lifelong ability to move forward, take control, and concentrate on others.

Although I have lived in a different universe, those experiences of my parents have always been compass points. They steer me to amusement when someone is sounding off, inflated by his own self-importance, to discomfort when I spend foolishly, to remorse when I complain about minor inconveniences.

In her insightful and evocative book *Dakota: A Spiritual Geography,* Kathleen Norris writes eloquently about the contradictions and tensions in the Dakota cultures, "between hospitality and insularity, change and inertia . . . between hope and despair, between open hearts and closed minds."

I've also learned to keep in perspective the almost automatic resistance in my native land to outside influences and criticism, however constructive they may be, and to unconventional ideas before they're fully explained. I understand why Dakotans are defensive. The Dakotas are looked on by many as largely empty tracts of land, remote and all but uninhabitable. It's been forty years since I lived in

South Dakota, but I still hear, "You're from South Dakota? Wow, how did you get all the way to New York?" Or, on a day of particularly harsh winter weather: "Well, you're from South Dakota; you're used to this." One year an atlas-publishing company left out large chunks of the South and North Dakota maps, explaining it was just trying to save space, as if no one would notice.

On these occasions when South Dakota is mocked in some way, I feel the slight, even now, and it tightens my bond with those who chose to stay. I also know they haven't given up on me. They expect me to carry the banner somehow. I am not always up to their expectations, but I have never surrendered the assignment, for it is a constant reminder of how my current life continues to be shaped by the currents of my formative years four decades after I left South Dakota. Mother, I believe, thinks I make too much of those influences; but that coolness to self-analysis is part of the pragmatic culture from which I draw strength. It is reassuring to know that the connection persists, built on common experiences of hard work, family, and community.

I was born in the middle of a harsh winter,

on February 6, 1940, on my grandfather Jim Conley's birthday, in Webster, Day County, South Dakota. I began life on a historic hinge, just as the Great Depression was ending and just before the United States entered World War II. It was a time when many of the families on the northern prairie still had no electricity or indoor plumbing. Telephones were on party lines and the railroad was still the great engine of transportation.

It is fourteen hundred miles from South Dakota to where I live and work now, in New York City, which has been my home for more than a quarter of a century. The mileage is the most imprecise measurement of the distance I've traveled in the forty years I've been gone. In recent years, as I've reached certain thresholds—the age of sixty, becoming a grandparent, contemplating the back third of my life and leaving the news anchor job—I've come to understand how important those early influences of family, place, and values were in making this life possible. I also know never to take any of this for granted, as I still live with the influences of failure as well as of success. In this book, I am on a journey of discovery, inspired in part by Lewis and Clark, who pushed into the grassy plains in 1804. My goals are of course far more modest. I am making my own way by looking back across the same landscape, trying to determine how I got from there to here. It has been for me an evocative and instructive expedition. I could not be the man I am today without the boy I was yesterday, in a far-off place and a long time ago.

CHAPTER 2

Work

MY ADULT LIFE AS A JOURNALIST HAS been forty years of long hours, unconventional schedules, occasional danger, foreign travel, front-row seats at historic events. It has been honest, demanding, and rewarding work, but it is not the work of my ancestors. It has involved almost no manual labor, whereas in the family and the culture in which I was raised, work defined lives, and the work that was especially admired and valued was physical labor that produced tangible, useful results. The ideal would be a man who could break the stubborn soil of the northern prairie, harvest a crop, butcher a cow, fix a fence, dig a well, build a house, and repair machinery; he would be married to a woman who could bake bread, plant a garden, hang out the wash, put up preserves, make soap, sew a family wardrobe, and nurse a sick child or a frail calf. The men and women in my family had done all of that.

Those myriad manual skills were required by the time, the land, and the climate in much of South Dakota. By the early sixties, when I left, the state's pioneer past had faded, along with the promise of family farm and ranch prosperity. Agriculture was going corporate, and the small towns that dotted the flat landscape were shrinking. By then I had my eye on the far horizon, wondering whether I could make my way beyond the rural culture that had nurtured me.

When I left, I was only vaguely aware of the demands and the hopes of the early days, when my great-grandfathers Richard Patterson Brokaw and Tom Conley settled in Day County, in the northern part of the state. Their projects seemed so promising, with the main line of the Milwaukee Road—the Chicago, Milwaukee, and St. Paul Railroad—running through the middle of thousands of acres of virgin grassland ready to be tilled and planted in wheat, barley, corn, and other small-grain crops. In the beginning their hard work paid real, if modest, rewards.

Dad atop a Caterpillar tractor in 1938.

When R. P. Brokaw arrived and helped lay out the town of Bristol, which had been called simply Section 70 by the railroad surveyors, he embodied the pioneer spirit. His son William, my grandfather, had been born in a covered wagon while R.P. and his wife made their way across the Dakota Territory. R.P. began construction of the Brokaw House hotel in the early 1880s, still several years before the final chapter of the notorious Indian Wars: the massacre of Sioux men, women, and children at Wounded Knee in southwestern South Dakota in 1890.

The three-story Brokaw House quickly became a town landmark, a smoky, noisy place, popular with itinerant railroad men and traveling salesmen who, for the benefit of local merchants, displayed their goods on long tables in a sample room just off the lobby. I remember that there were forty-five rooms for guests on the two upper floors. The Brokaw House anchored one end of Main Street, and by my father's recollection, most big events in Bristol began there: the Memorial Day parade, the annual dinner for the volunteer firemen, and the Fourth of July celebration.

R. P. Brokaw died in 1909. His son William

My grandfather William Brokaw and grandmother Elizabeth on their wedding day.

and daughter-in-law Elizabeth became the proprietors, but it was Elizabeth who did most of the work. Bill, as Dad's father was known, liked to patrol Bristol's main street as a policeman and spend hours in the lobby playing cribbage.

In the 1940s, when I was a toddler, the Brokaw House was also my home. My parents would return there in the winter when my father's construction work was put on hold until the spring. The old hotel informs some of my first memories and serves as a bridge between the lives of my parents and my own life. Mother and Dad converted a few of the rooms into their own small apartment, and I became the object of a great deal of affectionate attention from the permanent clientele.

The hotel—and most of its inhabitants—were born in the nineteenth century, and it had an old-fashioned aura, as if it were a holdover from another time. It was like nothing else in my world, and I never failed to experience a sense of adventure when I walked into its lobby or the always busy kitchen. I wasn't exactly Eloise at the Plaza, but I was already a talkative child and I relished being part of an extended family in a setting that was

My grandfather James Conley,
a pharmaceutical student
in Minneapolis.

much more like a large rooming house than a conventional hotel. I sometimes think that almost sixty years later I can still smell the cigar smoke from the lobby with its large pots of philodendrons and sturdy oak chairs. The reception desk was located beneath a flight of stairs leading to the second and third floors. The handsome French-made wall clock with a plate-sized brass oval at the end of a long pendulum that hung from one lobby wall now ticks quietly in my Montana home, another reminder of the passage of so much more than seconds, minutes, and hours.

The guests were mostly men, many with thick mustaches and large, gnarled hands, who dressed in denim overalls and flannel shirts. There were always a few of them sitting in the lobby, watching the passing traffic on Main Street with only a few scattered comments, as befitted their rural German and Scandinavian backgrounds. In the small cafés along Main Street they were known for "saucering" their coffee, spilling it from the cup into the saucer to cool it and then slurping it through their mustaches, which they wiped clean with a swipe of their large hands.

It was a functional place, with no frills or

Red, about the time he dropped out of school to go to work full-time, at the age of ten.

My dad, Red Brokaw— a tough guy with a tender heart.

unnecessary trimmings. Still, fire was a constant worry, especially with the heavy smoking habits of the guests. I remember being awakened early one morning by my mother, who said we had to get downstairs, fast. Smoke was everywhere. As I went down the stairs, I saw a guest going the other way, hauling a heavy fire extinguisher. Apparently a cigarette had started a mattress fire, and it was in danger of spreading. The men living at the hotel extinguished the fire well before Bristol's volunteer fire department arrived, which gave my brusque Aunt Leona a chance to stand at the lobby's large bay window and wave away, disgustedly, the tardy firemen. When Bill Brokaw died in 1943, Leona, the eldest daughter, became the hotel manager and straw boss of the family. She often greeted me, when I was just three years old or so, with the challenge "Put 'em up, c'mon, let's see how tough you are," and we'd exchange a few good-natured swings.

Ann and Celia, my father's other sisters, were single and worked at the local creamery, separating the milk from the cream and making butter. As a tot, I wondered why no one else seemed to notice that they came home from a shift carrying a faint odor of sour milk in their

Grandpa Jim Conley and a favorite dog,
just before the Great Depression, 1929.

My mother, Jean (on the left), with her cousin
Muriel, visiting the Conley farm, 1923.

all-white work uniforms. Now I realize that since the smell was the consequence of their jobs, it wasn't objectionable. The fact that they were hardworking, God-fearing, and fun-loving was much more important than a little odor, arrived at honestly.

Dad was the youngest of nine surviving children, three girls and six boys. His brothers left the hotel for better jobs or the military at early ages. In fact, all but two of them were gone by 1926, when Red was an adolescent. Four of the nine—two brothers and two sisters—never married.

The Brokaw siblings got along fine, but theirs was not what you'd call a close-knit family; the siblings shared a need to make their own way in the world and the trait of stubborn pride. They rarely asked for help or, God forbid, advice. Their economic circumstances also forced them to work hard from the time they were very young. Apart from my uncle Clarence, who collected antique glassware and china, none had hobbies or many recreational interests.

Every day was one form of drudgery or another, although they would never have called it that. Later in his life my father

*My father (on the far left), the youngest of the
Brokaw clan, with Celia, Richard, John, Ann,
Leona, Clifford, Clarence, and Lloyd. Note
the size of their hands.*

described his mother's daily ordeal of cooking for the hotel guests. Elizabeth started early, around 5:30 A.M., preparing hearty breakfasts of eggs, pancakes, oatmeal, bacon, and ham. Later in the day she was back in the tiny kitchen, firing up the coal stove to cook dinners that included roast beef or turkey, fried chicken, mashed potatoes, beets, peas, succotash, string beans, soups, coleslaw, salad, even shucked oysters, which came packed in salt in large barrels on the Milwaukee Road trains from Seattle. Each kind of vegetable was served in its own dish, so just keeping up with the crockery was a frantic task. When my father was eight or nine he was often pressed into service to help with the dishwashing, a demanding physical regimen.

Hot water came out of a fifty-gallon tank, the "waterback," attached to the coal stove. It had to be filled with five-gallon pails, heated, and then emptied daily for washing the dishes. The dirty dishwater was then hauled out to the backyard cistern, and the waterback was filled again for the next meal. The coal stove also had to be emptied of ashes and refilled for the next day's repetition of the grueling routine.

When he was not in the kitchen helping his

The Brokaw House.

R. P. Brokaw, Proprietor.

SUNDAY, DEC. 14, 1902.

✳ ✳

Oyster Stew.　　　　　Cold Slaw.

———

Celery.　　　　　　　　Olives.

———

Roast Turkey, with Dressing and Cranberry Sauce.

Domestic Duck with Spiced Apples.

Roast Beef, au Jus.

Boiled Lamb with Mushroom Sauce.

Strawberry Shortcake with Whipped Cream.

Tongue Salad.

———

Mashed Potatoes.　　　　　　　　Succotash.

Peas.　　　　　　　Squash.

———

Brown Bread.　　　　　　White Bread.

Steamed Brown Bread.

———

Steamed Suet Pudding, with Brandy Sauce.

———

Mince Pie.　　　　Apple Pie.　　　　Custard Pie.

Blueberry Pie.　　　　Orange Pudding.

———

Vanilla Ice Cream.　　　　　Assorted Cake.

———

Saratoga Flakes.　　　　　　　　Cheese.

———

Tea.　　　　　　Coffee.　　　　　　Milk.

PRice 50¢

A Sunday dinner at the Brokaw House, 1902.

mother, my dad, strong and large for his age, did chores assigned by his father. The coal for the stove was shipped in by rail from North Dakota. It was carried from the train to the hotel by horse-drawn wagon and then muscled onto the chutes leading to the basement. Dad remembered, matter-of-factly, "We had trouble sometimes. Some of those chunks of coal weighed a hundred pounds or more." Once the coal was stored, it was time to set aside fuel for the hotel furnace, so my grandfather would buy a load of railroad ties, maybe a hundred or so at a time.

At a time when he should have been in the fourth or fifth grade, Dad—along with his brother Rich, four years older—was cutting those railroad ties into shorter chunks for the furnace. They used a buck saw, a big two-man saw, to cut each tie into three or four pieces. Many of the ties were especially difficult to cut through because they had been treated with creosote to preserve them or were laced with sand absorbed from the railroad bed.

Before refrigeration, keeping perishables cool also required backbreaking labor. Ice arrived by railroad car in huge blocks which were offloaded and carried to the hotel, again in a horse-drawn wagon. Dad's job was to lead the team of horses on those cold winter days and help position the cakes of ice in a subterranean shed, where they lay covered in sawdust to preserve them as long as possible. In winter months a cake of ice, about 125 pounds, would last three or four days, but during the summer Dad and his brother would have to wrestle a big block out of the ice house every day or so, dragging it up with a rope on a pulley and loading it onto a two-wheeled wagon for the trip to the kitchen.

I remember the excitement when our family bought its first freezer, in about 1953. We plugged it in and within hours we were able to freeze vegetables from our garden for the winter and chickens, purchased from a local farmer, which Dad butchered and packaged. I wonder whether, as he stood looking at the new Kelvinator deep-freeze, he flashed back to those blocks of ice.

A permanent guest at the Brokaw House was a Swedish immigrant, Oscar Johnson. A bachelor, Oscar had at some point been a homesteader on the bleak prairie of western South Dakota, a semi-arid landscape where even now modern agriculture struggles to break even.

How long Oscar tried to make it there I am not sure, but somehow he worked his way back to Bristol, where he bought some land, a few cows, and a horse and established a small well-digging and moving company. I can still see his room at the Brokaw House. It had a simple iron-frame bed and one bureau, and there was a long string leading from the lone lightbulb in the center of the ceiling through a series of eye hooks on a route that led to a position just above Oscar's pillow. There were no other amenities in the room (the toilet was at the end of the hall).

My father was Oscar's most reliable (and often his only) employee, signing on at the age of ten shortly after he dropped out of school. No one in Dad's family seemed to object, and although he later regretted stopping his education so early, he was especially gifted in mechanics and the conceptual perception which is so critical to the building and construction trades. His hands and mind worked together with an artistry few could emulate. He was the model of a self-made man. In Oscar, he found a demanding but benevolent mentor.

When Dad's father got into financial trouble, the sheriff came to the hotel lobby to foreclose on the property. Dad, just a boy at the time, wondered where he would live. Oscar emerged from his room and told the sheriff he would pay off the debt. With that, Oscar became not just my dad's boss but also his surrogate father.

Oscar was a sinewy man, with large hands stained yellow by nicotine from a lifetime of smoking. When he smiled he showed off uneven rows of long, yellow teeth which probably had never been exposed to a dentist's tools. Oscar was a man of few words and, I believe, little formal education; he spoke with the distinctive sound of his native language until he died.

He cobbled together an income out of moving buildings, digging wells, repairing windmills, and raising hay and a few cows. His lifelong uniform was a pair of denim bib overalls, a work shirt, and sturdy boots. Every winter he bought a new pair of overalls and a new flannel shirt to wear over his long underwear; that would carry him through the year. He led a simple life of working, eating, and sleeping, with very few diversions.

That life became my father's boyhood when he joined up with Oscar. Together they spent long hours doing the brute labor of their trade;

they became a fixed part of the local landscape, Oscar and his tough little assistant. From the perspective of the twenty-first century, Oscar might seem to be a terrible exploiter of child labor, but I am sure his own childhood in rural Sweden was the model for his conduct. He'd had a hard life and he just expected everyone else would as well. It's unlikely that he thought twice about the demands he placed on the youngest Brokaw. The Roaring Twenties were in full throttle, and great industrial fortunes were being made, but in the heartland, which relied on a backbreaking economy, less than a quarter of the young men went on to high school.

Later, when Mother and Dad had started a family and we were living some distance from Bristol, Oscar arrived on short notice for a winter visit. By then he was stone deaf and certainly no more talkative. He sat for hours in our living room, paging through back copies of *Life* magazine and *The Saturday Evening Post* while my mother said aloud, confident he couldn't hear, "I wonder how long he's going to stay."

Providentially, a huge blizzard engulfed our town and there was a lot of snow to be removed. Oscar got up that morning, silently put on his mackinaw wool coat, thick pigskin mittens, wool cap, and four-buckle overshoes, and waded happily into the knee-deep snow, armed with a large scoop shovel. I trailed behind with a smaller shovel, and together we attacked the sidewalk in front of our house. He removed a yard of snow at a time with long, graceful strokes, working rhythmically until the cold numbed his hands, which had been frostbitten so often. Oscar would pause, smile at me, and suck in the cold air through those long teeth as he clapped his mittened hands to restore circulation. It was as if he were applauding the glories of nature and the rewards of honest work. I never fail to recall that scene when I see snow, although I am much more likely to be skiing on it or admiring its beauty than shoveling it.

With Oscar as his employer and silent mentor, Dad had a childhood of almost all work and very little play. He never owned his own bike and he rarely had time for baseball or the other normal pursuits of boyhood. I was deeply involved in all kinds of sports growing up and I occasionally wondered why he didn't invoke his own childhood athletic exploits. In fact, he had almost never had the time to play. Work came first, last, and always. Yet later in life he recalled the amusing or instructive moments much more than the long hours, the low pay, and the missed games.

One of Dad's favorite stories involved a job for a farmer who had lost some pipes down an old well and had called on Oscar and Dad to retrieve them. Oscar tied a rope around one of Dad's legs and lowered him headfirst into the deep, dark well, which could have collapsed at any moment. Hanging there, upside down, Dad—just ten years old—managed to collect the pipes and tie them. He was a muddy mess, so he changed into clean clothes. But just then the farm dog came running by, chasing some of the farmer's new little pigs. One of the piglets panicked and jumped into the well, landing in the water forty feet down.

That piglet was money on the hoof so, once again, Oscar tied a rope around Dad and down Dad went. He always laughed when he told the story. "If you don't think that's hard—hanging on to the slippery pig, coming up out of the well, and hanging on to the rope with the other hand . . . but somehow we got the pig out and everything went along well."

It was not unusual for Dad to take on dangerous jobs at such a young age. He ran a big old-fashioned mower behind a large team of horses in the hayfields, a demanding job even for a strong full-grown man. He sat on a precarious seat above the mower's axle, with the powerful blades rotating just behind as the horses were driven over the rough ground of a hayfield. If the horses stumbled or bolted, or if the rig hit a hole, the driver could easily be thrown into the mower's path.

Dad was a strong boy but still just a youngster, so his legs didn't reach the axle for balance. Oscar simply put a block of wood below the seat so Dad could brace his legs and get the job done. I am confident no one protested that this was an inappropriate risk for a boy. Later in life Dad was skeptical of the strictures imposed by OSHA, the federal Occupational Safety and Health Administration. I think he believed, on the basis of his own early experiences, that risk on the job was just something to be managed.

The demands on his labor at such a tender age left a lasting impression. Frozen in his memory was one winter night when Oscar hired him and his brother Richard, then fourteen to Dad's ten, to help move a building from the next town east.

The building had been jacked onto a wagon with iron wheels and a frame of large timbers, twelve inches by twelve inches and fifty feet long. Dad and Richard were each responsible for one of the two teams of horses that pulled the wagon. Half a century later, Dad remembered, "We were cold . . . we were watering the horses at a farm place when we heard the Webster whistle blow. It was six P.M. And of course it was twelve miles to Bristol."

They'd be walking alongside the horses through the frigid Dakota night. More than seventy-five years later, that stretch of road remains dark and lonely after the winter sun sets. Just a few years ago, a woman trying to get back to Webster during a blizzard got stuck in a drift, and although she had a cell phone it took searchers two days to find her. The two Brokaw brothers might have had wool mackinaws, and they probably wore long underwear, but they sure as hell didn't have much else, not headlamps or modern flashlights. They were on foot and very likely had not eaten since noon.

It was midnight when the two boys drove their teams into Bristol, parked the cumbersome wagon, and got the horses into the barn. When Dad recalled that night in oral memoirs he recorded for our family in 1980, he described it matter-of-factly, but for me the passage was poignant. I could see in my mind's eye these two little redheaded boys hurrying to unhitch the horses in the cold South Dakota night and running into the darkened hotel. Dad said that he and Richard were hungry but they just went to bed, keeping all their clothes on because there was no central heat upstairs in the hotel, only whatever came from the chimney and the downstairs cook stove.

Small wonder that Richard left Bristol at age sixteen to join the Coast Guard and then the Navy before settling in California. He returned to Bristol only for family vacations. And he became a leading Boy Scout troop leader in the Long Beach area, once turning out a record number of Eagle Scouts. Perhaps he was making up for his own missing boyhood.

On one of those bitterly cold nights after Richard was gone, Dad went to bed suffering from the flu after another long day. He recalled that he began to cry, feeling sorry for himself, and with good reason. His mother had died a short time before, when he was just twelve, and he felt utterly alone and longed for her comforting ways.

It was 1924. In New York that year, a new

company was formed by a National Cash Register executive, Thomas J. Watson. He named it International Business Machines—IBM for short. A new store, Saks Fifth Avenue, opened just south of St. Patrick's Cathedral and featured for sale a $3,000 pigskin trunk and $1,000 raccoon coats. In Chicago, the thirty-four-story Wrigley Building was completed. There were three million radio sets in the United States. A new car was introduced in Detroit, called the Chrysler.

America was booming, but that was of little comfort to twelve-year-old Red Brokaw. His sister Ann heard him crying from her room down the hall and brought heated lemonade to ward off the chills.

Until that point, Dad had slept in whatever room happened to be empty at bedtime. Ann wisely decided it was time for him to have a place of his own. She told him that from now on this would be his room, to fix up as he wanted. He was elated and immediately wrote his name in the small pine bureau against the wall. Five decades later, he refinished that little piece of his childhood and presented it to our youngest daughter, Sarah, for her New York room of *her* own.

But a room of one's own can't replace a

mother, and Dad's father wasn't much on parental love, so Red continued to do what he knew best: he worked. In the evening, after milking cows or stacking hay for the winter feeding, he often worked for the local movie-house owner, rounding up patrons for the silent films that made their way to Bristol, again via the railroad. He'd walk up and down Main Street shouting, "Two reels of a comedy tonight—and Tom Mix," ringing a handbell to attract attention, shouting into the crowded, smoky pool hall. Those days were the beginning of America's love affair with movies. By 1926, an estimated fifty million people a week were going to the movies; by 1930, that number had jumped to ninety million.

For that job, Dad was given free theater tickets, and since he didn't have school the next day, or anyone at home worrying about his whereabouts, he'd often stay for two features and then fall asleep in his seat. The theater manager would leave him there when time came to close for the night; when Dad awoke, he'd let himself out the back door and head for his cold room at the Brokaw House.

In that God-fearing community of well-ordered German and Scandinavian families, where discipline and deportment were a fixed part of life, the young, tough, red-haired Brokaw boy was the odd kid out, the local tough guy. Other mothers were leery of letting their children play with a boy who didn't go to school or church, who smoked from age ten on, and who welcomed farm kids to town by chasing them through the streets, challenging them to a fight.

One Sunday, however, he confronted his reputation in his own way. He'd been visiting a farm family south of town, riding horses with other boys. One of the visitors had a minor horse wreck and injured his knee. A storm was brewing, so the mother at the farm told the boys they'd better spend the night. She dutifully called the injured boy's parents to let them know where he was and that he'd be okay. Dad couldn't help but notice that she didn't bother to call his family because she assumed, correctly, no one would notice he was missing.

The next day she questioned Dad closely about his school and religious habits. When he told her the closest he got to church was when "I drive the cows by the Lutheran church in the morning about the time they ring the bell," she was stern and disapproving. No doubt speaking for most of the mothers in town, she said, "That's awful, growing up that way." But she didn't offer to help.

So Dad decided to help himself, and he did so by using his considerable skills and energy to do good work for others. Later in life, as he recalled this epiphany, Dad wrote, "I always got blamed for everything that went wrong in town, even when I was out working in the country with Oscar. So I made up my mind I was going to show them that I was better than their kids."

Dad made himself into the local Good Samaritan. He delivered coal and soft water to the elderly at half his normal rate. "I was supposed to get forty cents for a load of coal—a ton. Twenty cents for hauling it—twenty cents for unloading it. But I'd charge just for the unloading of it." Or if a widow he knew couldn't pay even the twenty cents, he'd deliver the coal anyway, knowing she needed it and would pay eventually.

It was a pattern he maintained throughout his life. I still hear about his generosity—the unexpected gift of a handmade bassinet for a couple expecting their first child, or napkin rings he carved for a friend from a piece of black walnut he had milled, or the hours he spent helping a young friend overhaul the engine on a secondhand car. He had a big heart for those he thought worthy. But for those who slighted him or put on airs, well, the Brokaw stubborn streak was a formidable force.

Once, as a young man, Dad agreed to deliver a load of coal to a Bristol banker, an aloof figure and a man of great power in that small town. After shoveling the load of coal into the banker's basement, about a ton altogether, Dad dusted the top of the coal pile with a light sprinkling of snow. This was, he explained, his ingenious way of keeping the coal dust to a minimum. The banker had his own ideas and ran out into the yard demanding loudly that the snow be removed. Red Brokaw probably didn't have a bank account or expect to do any business with the bank anytime soon, but even if he had, I am confident his reaction would have been the same. He laughed when he remembered that he not only removed the light layer of snow, he emptied the basement of the newly delivered coal and drove off with it, leaving the banker to make other arrangements for his winter fuel.

Such experiences built up in him a lifetime

of animosity toward small-minded authority figures. His early years made him a true populist, someone who was never in awe of power, especially when it came dressed in a white shirt, suit, and tie.

He expressed his admiration for values that had meaning to his own life of struggle. For example, since he didn't have time for baseball or football as a kid, he was never a big sports fan, never devoted to one team or another or to a particular player. Yet he often held up two sports figures to me as role models, not because of their athletic prowess but because of their other attributes. One was Gene Tunney, the heavyweight boxing champion who gained power with fists and then had the intelligence to retire with his money and his senses intact. The other was Jesse Owens, who gave Hitler—and America—a lesson in race when he won four gold medals at the 1936 Olympic Games in record time and with world-class grace.

A few years after his encounter with the stern farm woman, Dad had another life-changing moment. This one involved two sorrel colts that came up for sale at an auction. Oscar agreed to finance their purchase—$40 for the pair of young horses. For Dad, it was the bargain of a lifetime. He dressed the colts in hand-decorated bridles and reins and quickly made them into a cash business.

They were his bread and butter. He became an all-purpose delivery man, bringing coal, water, and freight and meeting the other requirements of small-town commerce. When a contractor came through Bristol, working on the highway, he tried to rent the team to supplement his small force of machinery. Dad struck a bargain that defined his future and lifted him out of the rut of Bristol's low-paid manual labor: he told the contractor he would rent the horses only if he too was part of the deal.

He got twenty cents an hour for the horses and forty cents an hour for himself. It was the most money he'd ever made. "So, my goodness," he remembered, "there I was making sixty cents an hour. Otherwise I was lucky if I was making fifty cents a day in that town." He was also working hard, doing whatever the contractor asked of him, from chopping trees to sloping the highway banks by hand.

One day a foreman came charging up. Dad was afraid he was about to be fired, but instead the foreman asked, "Anyone here ever run a

Caterpillar?" Dad and one of his friends volunteered to learn how to operate that big earth-moving tractor. For Red Brokaw, it was the equivalent of winning the lottery. Some people have a natural feel for numbers, words, or music. Dad, it turned out, was a man of machines. When he stepped onto that Caterpillar it was a perfect match, and that was the beginning of his way out of the constraints of the economic opportunities in Bristol.

By the end of the summer, the contractor had other work for Dad, 170 miles away in Minnesota. To get there, Dad had to drive one of the lumbering steel-tracked Caterpillars on back roads of gravel or packed dirt. It took a week to make the trip. He always had fond memories of the journey, but it must have been a chore. "I rented rooms in farmhouses along the way and by the time I got there I couldn't hear a word, from that rumbling old Cat," he remembered.

Those experiences, combined with a congenital hearing problem in the Brokaw clan, left Dad nearly deaf later in life, but he never complained. He had just been happy to have the work.

About the same time, Dad took up roller-skating and motorcycling, primarily to make money. He was in a small troupe that performed trick routines on roller skates in local variety shows for cash prizes, and on weekends he often entered motorcycle hill climbs, borrowing his brother John's motorcycle. But these were mercenary diversions; he never took up roller-skating or motorcycling again just for pleasure.

His pals from that time also recall with great amusement the time a touring professional boxer came through, looking for some local action. Dad was known as the toughest guy in town, so his friends persuaded him into the ring. But Red was strictly an untrained street brawler, and it wasn't long after the opening bell that the Minneapolis boxer landed a solid punch and knocked him out. Dad got $5 for the effort, and his buddies got a lifetime of hilarity.

Southwest of Bristol, Eugenia Conley, Jean, had been growing up on the family farm. She walked to a one-room country schoolhouse, carrying her lunch in an empty Karo syrup can. She was a precocious dark-haired child with a sister seven years younger, a bookish father who was a bit of a dreamer, and a mother who had given up the middle-class comforts of Minneapolis for the demands of farm life on a treeless prairie.

Jean Conley often worked beside her father as he planted the corn and wheat, hauled the hay, milked the cows, and fed the pigs, chickens, and turkeys they raised. She especially enjoyed their horse and sled rides across the snowy prairie on clear, cold winter nights when her father, always the teacher, would point out the Milky Way, the Big Dipper, and the Northern Lights. It was the life so familiar to readers of Laura Ingalls Wilder's *Little House on the Prairie,* updated to the early twentieth century.

Her childhood on the farm south of Bristol was at once adventurous and difficult, although she always preferred to remember the adventures. For the first seven years of her life she was Jim and Ethel's only child. Their small house had neither electricity nor indoor plumbing. The hired man lived in a loft above the family quarters.

The Conleys were at the tail end of a farming boom in America. In 1914, about 30 percent of Americans worked in agriculture, but that figure dropped to about 25 percent by 1920. Still, in the early twenties, when America was enjoying a post–World War I boom, the family farm was a promising if not wildly profitable enterprise.

Jim was able to get decent prices for his grain, and their other labors paid off on Saturday nights, when they drove to town in their Model T Ford loaded with crates of turkeys, cartons of eggs, and bushels of fresh vegetables for sale or to barter with local merchants for store-bought goods. Those early lessons in commerce left a lifelong impression on Mother. To this day she often instinctively rattles off the price of each dish as she serves dinner. "Can you believe it? I got these beautiful pork chops, two for $2.95. And I couldn't pass up these big strawberries. They were on sale."

There was very little cash in her childhood, but the close rural community provided rich and lasting lessons in resourcefulness and cooperation. Those 160-acre farms made up a tightly woven fabric on the northern prairie. Neighbors were close by, and in the winter months families often visited each other, steering their teams of horses and sleighs across open fields covered with snow.

One of the locals was an inventive sort, so a

gathering at his house meant more than just the usual round of gossip and card playing. Mother remembers that he had assembled a rope-making machine and set it up in his kitchen. The men spent their day off talking over prices and local politics and making rope. The same neighbor also had a shoe repair bench so boots and shoes could be resoled for another season's wear. Do-it-yourself was not a Martha Stewart fashion but a necessity.

My grandmother Ethel had been raised in Minneapolis, where her father had a substantial job as a foreman at one of the large Pillsbury flour mills. The adjustment to the barren prairie and farm life was not easy, even when their new two-story home was constructed. In her first few years it was not unusual for my grandfather to come in from the fields and find Ethel with her bags packed, desperate for a trip back to the Twin Cities.

After a week or so she'd return to the hard life in South Dakota, overcoming her loneliness by keeping busy with the many chores required to feed and clothe the family while also attending to her part of the farm business. Mother recorded just some of the jobs that this city girl had in her new life: churning butter by hand; boiling large tubs of water for the laundry, which was then hung outside, winter and summer alike; ironing, a daylong job that required stoking the coal range to heat the heavy primitive irons. And when Jim Conley butchered a hog or cow, Ethel was at his side, rendering the fat into lard, canning the meat.

All the hot water for cooking, bathing, and other indoor and outdoor use was heated on the Majestic, the large black stove that also doubled as an incubator for baby chicks and piglets. It was also the cookstove for soups, casseroles, homemade bread, porridge, and the other staples of the rural diet. That nutritional regimen, supplemented with regular doses of castor oil, must have been effective: Mother was named "Healthiest Girl in Day County" when she was in the eighth grade. Her photo in the Webster paper was a portrait of vibrant youth. She won the title despite resisting her father's daily insistence that she eat her oatmeal porridge for strong bones and a long life.

In the wintertime, Mother did her home-work near the stove, often with her feet propped up on the open oven door for warmth. I often think that Grandmother Ethel must have run that Majestic as an engineer would have run a coal-burning locomotive.

Mother grew up quickly as she worked

beside her parents in the house, the farmyard, and the fields. At the one-room schoolhouse a mile up the road, she mixed easily with the older students. Her teachers decided she could skip a grade, so by the time Jim Conley lost the farm and moved the family to town, Jean was well ahead of her age.

When Dad was twenty and Mother fifteen, he went to a school play in Bristol and took special notice of her on stage. Dad bet a friend he could get a date with her, an uncharacteristically bold offer on two counts: he had almost no confidence in his social skills with women, and since he worked so hard for his money, he almost never gambled.

How he won the bet and eventually won Jean's heart is now part of family lore. "I had never even said hello to your mother," he told us later. He described how he parked outside the Conley house: "I left the lights on in the car. I left the motor running. When she came to the door, I stuttered and stammered and I asked her if she wanted to go to the show in Webster with a bunch of us. I think I kind of took her by surprise, and she actually went along."

It was an unlikely pairing. Jean Conley was

from a tight-knit family with very protective parents. She was as gregarious as Red Brokaw was shy, and she loved school, which had given him such trouble. Much later, when I asked what she saw in him, she said, "Oh, he was good-looking, polite, he had a great sense of humor, and he always had a little extra money so we could do things. He was always respect-ful around me and my parents; if someone tried to tell an off-color joke in our company, he'd cut them off. My dad liked him, and thought he would do well."

But even with that little extra money, it was hardly a champagne-and-flowers courtship. Jean and Red dated in a car full of other friends, all going to the same movie or the same dance. This went on for almost two years, until Jean moved to the nearby small town of Andover for her senior year in high school. The move was dictated by the family's precarious finances; it was the height of the Depression, and Jim Conley had found an inexpensive two-bedroom house to rent.

The first time Dad came calling there, they sat in his car and realized they had never been alone before. They found themselves awkward and unable to say much. I am always moved by that scene—the two of them in Dad's car, shy and uncertain, knowing only that they cared for each other. I am certain Dad saw in Mother the woman of his dreams, someone who would help him rise above his childhood reputation as a dead-end kid. It was about then that he began to confide in her his determination to amount to something beyond his odd jobs around Bristol.

Jean—Mother—was working as a waitress at a local café, earning a dime an hour plus her meals. She had hoped to go to college and become a teacher, but that would cost $125 a year, well beyond her limited means. However, her upbringing on the farm had made her self-reliant and enterprising. She also worked at the local post office for a dollar a day. The postmaster would pay her at the end of each day with the same well-meant but tired line: "There you are, Jean, a million days, a million dollars."

By the time she was dating Dad, they both had an appreciation of hard work, self-reliance, and self-esteem. It was an unspoken part of their mutual attraction and it defined their lives forevermore. They were married in July 1938, and when they left the next day for Minnesota, where Dad had landed a construction job, they had surveying rods tied alongside their honeymoon car. Dad's skill with earth-moving equipment and his diligence kept him in work during those difficult times in the construction industry, even though employment dropped by half.

That one-day honeymoon and the race to the next job were a metaphor for Mother and Dad's lives and the way they raised their three sons. They combined practicality and productivity in every aspect of their lives. They passed along those values more by personal example than by lecture. Mother and Dad were always going off to work or busy on some project at home. When they commented on the good fortune of a friend's son, they'd often say, in a quiet, meaningful way, "He has a *good* job," meaning with some company that offered security and benefits.

They took pride in their well-ordered lawns and flower gardens, but I cannot remember them simply sitting for long in the lawn chairs that Dad built, kicking off their shoes and taking in what they had accomplished. Moreover, no project was ever deferred. It was a house rule that was sometimes a strain on my brothers and me.

One Friday night when I was playing high

school basketball I had an uncharacteristically productive game and I couldn't wait to get to the local hangout to receive the accolades. But I made the mistake of stopping by home first. Dad was on a ladder in the small dining area, beginning the framework for installing acoustical tiles on the ceiling. It was 9:30 on a Friday night and he had worked a full week, but this was a project he had on his calendar and so, by God, he was going to do it.

He lured me into helping him get the job started. Laughing, he kept me on a short leash: "Just help me a few more minutes here." "Hand me that stapler." I began to protest, but it was no use. We finished well after midnight and my night of glory was converted into a lesson in installing acoustical tile.

For her part, Mother made it clear that she was not going to spend all her hours trying to keep up with the laundry needs of three boys. We were all taught to wash and iron shirts and pants and to make minor repairs with needle and thread. I still find myself in a fancy hotel suite, summoning an ironing board and iron so I can press some item of clothing rather than pay the outrageous price and go through the inconvenience of waiting for it to be returned from valet service.

Work remains central to my life—in spare moments I am not inclined to just kick back and stare off into space; I am constantly reviewing chores to finish and projects to begin—but the skills that go with much of manual labor, I have learned, are not genetically encoded. My father had an intuitive sense of mechanics and construction; I do not.

I can identify most tools in a carpenter's or mechanic's inventory and I take pride in using them correctly from time to time. But the fit is not natural. When I set out on a household task like rewiring a lamp socket or assembling a plant stand, I am likely to engage in a kind of dialogue with my father, now dead almost twenty years: "Okay, Red, where does this go?" It's one of the ways I stay in touch with him.

I also keep in my small collection of fundamental tools a large hammer. It has a plain, heavy head, very simple in design. It was sent to me a few years ago by a man from Oregon who explained that he had grown up in South Dakota as a friend of my father's. He borrowed the hammer from Dad sometime in the 1920s and never got around to returning it. He explained that he'd replaced the handle many times and that the hammer had been in almost constant use for seventy-five years. He wanted me to have it.

I consider it an heirloom, a symbol of my heritage as an offspring of working men and women.

CHAPTER 3

Boom Times

ONCE THEY WERE MARRIED AND MOV-
ing from job to job across the Midwest, from
Minnesota to Kansas, building highways and
airports, Mother and Dad lived in rooming
houses and small trailers during the spring,
summer, and fall, returning to the Brokaw
House to wait out the harsh winter.

It was during one of those winters, on February 6, 1940, that I was born in Webster, the
Day County seat, twelve miles from Bristol.
February 6 was also my grandfather Jim's
birthday. The birth of a son to Jean and Red
was a joyous time for my parents and their families but an ominous time in the world, with
Hitler ruthlessly expanding his Nazi empire
throughout Europe, while in the Pacific the

*My grandma Ethel, Aunt Marcia, my mother, and
me in Grandpa Conley's arms, on the day Marcia
graduated from high school, May 1941.*

Japanese had their own fanatical imperialistic designs.

Throughout much of America, including the conservative Midwest, the sentiment was overwhelmingly against U.S. involvement in the fight against either power. Ideologically and geographically, a majority of Americans felt far removed from the threats East and West. Pearl Harbor on December 7, 1941, changed all that; by the time I was conscious of my surroundings, America was at war.

My earliest memories are of a summer we spent in a lake cottage outside Alexandria, Minnesota, where my father was helping build a new airport. The cottage had an old-fashioned icebox and no indoor plumbing, but it was a toddler's delight. The lake was just a few feet from the screened-in porch, and the neighborhood was filled with children ranging from my age to the early teens. The lake was chock-full of easy-to-catch panfish—crappies, bluegills, and sunfish—as well as large snapping turtles that would occasionally make their way across our lawn. Mother and Dad and the other young families from the construction crew organized regular picnics of fried chicken, potato salad, Jell-O, watermelon, and

The Brokaw brothers at the Army Ordnance Depot in Igloo, South Dakota, 1944.

the other staples of that Norman Rockwell summer meal of the heartland.

My father and the other men were in their late twenties or early thirties and waiting for their numbers to come up in the military draft. The war seemed a long way from the Minnesota lake country, but when night fell there were often blackouts: all lights were shut off so any enemy bombers that made their way fifteen hundred miles into the American interior wouldn't have easy targets. Looking back, I suspect the real reason for the blackouts was to remind everyone that the war was on, more than to confuse enemy bombers.

Late that fall, when I was just two and a half years old but already a wanderer, I joined some older children on a dock to splash the now chilly lake water on a brave youngster who was wading near the shore. My mother thought I was in the care of a baby-sitter. Suddenly, and I can see it even now, I was tumbling through the water, bubbles rising toward the surface. I had fallen off the end of the dock into water well over my head.

The next thing I remember is a young girl handing me off to my mother. I was screaming and soaked, terrified and confused. My mother was, understandably, practically in a state of shock. The girl was not from the neighborhood but had happened by and dove in to rescue me. She disappeared after delivering me to our cottage, and we never did learn her name. It was the beginning of a lifetime of close calls and lucky breaks.

By then I had a baby brother, Bill, ten months old, and Mother was expecting a third child in a few months. Dad heard about a job at a new Army ordnance depot—a storage facility for bombs and artillery shells—scraped out of the sagebrush hills of southwestern South Dakota. The base was called Igloo, after the ordnance storehouses on the arid landscape that were shaped like Eskimo igloos. The U.S. Army Corps of Engineers was responsible for making sure the base functioned smoothly, and Dad was hired at $6.88 a day.

As he awaited his call to service, Red worked at keeping the new base operating, plowing snow, building roads to the storage bunkers, repairing the fleet of cars and trucks, all painted U.S. Army olive green. When his draft notice arrived, he passed his physical and planned to enlist in the Navy. He thought his skills would be best used in the Navy's construction branch, the Seabees.

But the colonel running the ordnance depot called Red back, saying he was more important to that facility than he would be in the Navy. So I had a stay-at-home dad for the remainder of the war, one who was making his contribution in civilian clothing rather than a military uniform. He was thirty-two at the time.

As for me, I had never known any time when the country was not at war and I suppose I thought it would go on forever. At ages three, four, and five I was shooting imaginary Japanese and German soldiers from the cover of a shallow ditch in front of our small government house on the base. My "weapon" was a wooden gun my father had carved out a piece of scrap lumber.

Most of our toys were handmade, as toy production was put on hold for the war effort. One Christmas, almost every present for the Brokaw boys had been handcrafted by our father or one of his fellow workers at the shop, as they called the large garage where they reported to work daily. We got a wooden wagon, carved wooden cars, and a toy pistol turned out in the metalworking shop.

Forty years later I returned to what remained of Igloo with my parents and my own daughters. We found the foundation of our old house, which had a coal stove in the living room for heat and an old-fashioned wood-burning cookstove on which Mother prepared meals and heated water for baby brother Mike's baths in a washtub. Dad and his granddaughter Sarah, our youngest child, walked off the foundation and estimated that the entire house was twenty feet by twenty feet, about the size of her bedroom in our New York apartment.

While Dad was at work in Igloo, Mother was at home with three boys under the age of four. My youngest brother, Mike, had been born at the base, just fifteen months after Bill. We were confined to that small space during the harsh winter months, and yet I cannot recall any sense of hardship or any bickering between my parents. As my mother likes to remind me, "Everyone was in the same boat."

My entire world, from the surrounding arid hills to the uniforms and vehicles, was khaki brown or olive green—except for some strangers confined to a stockade on the edge of Igloo, who wore bright orange uniforms and spoke a strange language in rapidfire fashion. They were Italian prisoners who had been shipped a long way from the front lines of southern Europe to sit out the war in South Dakota.

Security was not exactly airtight; the POWs were allowed to wander through town on their low-grade job assignments, mowing lawns, picking up litter, and working as orderlies in the hospital. Many years later, Mother confided to me that a few of them struck up romantic liaisons with war widows.

Curiously, although I recall so much of a child's life from that time—sledding in winter, fishing trips, the movie *Song of the South,* the names of playmates and my kindergarten teacher, even the whipped cream the police chief's wife, a nurse, served on their Jell-O desserts—I have no specific memory of the death of Franklin Roosevelt. FDR was a demigod to my parents and grandparents, so it must have been a terrible blow when he died in 1945. But, perhaps because the news came by radio—so it was not visual—it failed to register on my five-year-old consciousness. I do remember, though only vaguely, the celebrations when the war was over. Edgemont, a

tough little ranching town next to the ordnance base, was where the young soldiers went
to drink and gamble and it was there they
spilled out onto Main Street to raucously toast
the victories.

Shortly after the celebrations marking, first,
the victory in Europe—VE Day—and then the
defeat of Japan—VJ Day—ended, the sounds of
construction created a welcome cacophony
across America. In 1940, there were slightly
more than 23.7 million single-family homes in
America; by 1950, another 5.5 million had
been constructed and by 1960 the total had
jumped to more than 40 million.

America was shifting gears rapidly, changing
from a war machine to the most powerful
domestic economy in the world. For four years,
Detroit had been turning out tanks, warplanes,
jeeps, and heavy all-terrain trucks for ferrying
troops and supplies to the front lines. From 3.7
million cars manufactured in 1941, Detroit
went to just over 200,000 the next year and
none in 1943 and 1944. When car production
resumed, in 1945, it came back with a roar. In
1949 production reached more than 5.1 mil-

lion, a number that rose to more than 6.6 million the following year.

When Dwight Eisenhower became president, in 1952, he was enthusiastic about an initiative started during the Roosevelt years, a national highway construction program. This was a critical component in making America a modern economic power, and in those postwar years the importance of good roads for military purposes was also a consideration. By 1956 the Federal Highway Act was in place, a program that led to 42,800 miles of modern highways connecting all regions of the country. In his memoirs, Ike said, "More than any single action by the government since the end of the war, this one would change the face of America."

When the war was over, Dad and Mother decided to play it safe. We were now five, and the idea of packing three kids into the back of the family car, a 1939 Ford sedan, and striking out for more seasonal work in a strange state didn't hold much appeal.

They'd been hearing about a massive construction scheme planned for South Dakota. It was the Pick-Sloan Project, four large dams to be built across the Missouri River for flood control and hydroelectricity. The U.S. Army Corps of Engineers was in charge and, in the can-do spirit of the times, the Corps didn't worry much about environmental impact or long-term economic consequences. An eager constituency in the U.S. Congress was enthusiastic about the Corps' big plans and the big momentum coming out of the war, especially in small rural states such as South Dakota, which weren't going to cash in on the manufacturing boom under way in California, Ohio, Pennsylvania, Michigan, and the other industrial giants.

For my parents, true children of the Depression, there was another substantial attraction: Although government wages were half what Red could earn atop a bulldozer or road grader working for a private contractor, federal employees had job benefits and security, especially those who had already accumulated strong records as U.S. Army Corps of Engineers workers during the war.

My parents decided to work on the dam planned for a remote section of the river in south-central South Dakota, at a place where the 7th Cavalry once had an outpost called Fort Randall. The area was mostly farmland and the reservation of the Yankton Sioux, a small tribe of that Indian nation. Significant portions of the reservation land had been sold to white farmers, and the Yanktons were scattered along the Missouri bottomland, living in small cabins or in the nearby farming communities, almost always in their own neighborhoods.

The Yankton were the first Sioux that Lewis and Clark encountered when they entered that section of the Great Plains in late August 1804. In their journals, the explorers recount a friendly meeting with several Yankton chiefs, including the head man, Weucha, whose name translates as Shake Hand.

After being given medals and a U.S. flag, Weucha, as recorded in the Lewis and Clark journals, said to the explorers—who had been sent by Thomas Jefferson—"I see before me my great father's two sons. You see me and the rest of our chiefs and warriors. We are very poor; we have neither powder nor ball nor knives, and our women and children at the village have no clothes. I wish that as my brothers have given me a flag and a medal, they would have given something to those poor people, or let them stop and trade with the first boat that comes up the river."

When the Brokaw family arrived in Yankton

territory less than 150 years later, little had changed. The tribe was still poor and not much of a force in the agricultural economy developed by late-nineteenth-century immigrants from Scandinavia and central Europe, particularly, in this corner of the state, Czechoslovakia.

Fort Randall Dam, when completed, was to be the largest earth-rolled dam in the world, a two-mile-long berm anchored by a massive concrete powerhouse with eight state-of-the-art electric turbines and a concrete spillway the size of two football fields. It would take almost ten years of year-round construction to complete, and that meant thousands of workers would be pouring into an area of small farming villages. A new town had to be built quickly.

Mother's parents, Jim and Ethel Conley, had preceded us in the search for postwar work. They were settled into a trailer house parked on the edge of a baseball diamond in Wagner, South Dakota, the largest community in Charles Mix County. It was twelve miles from where the new dam would be built; my grandfather was hired by one of the contractors involved in the initial excavation. My maternal grandparents spent the rest of their lives in trailer parks, a cozy and economical arrangement for them. I always bristle when I hear the phrase "trailer trash" or any of its degrading variations.

We five Brokaws followed Jim and Ethel to this new promised land in the trusty Ford sedan, hauling a two-wheel trailer packed with a few pieces of furniture, kitchen utensils, and our functional but not elaborate wardrobe.

In later years, when I recalled the move, Mother would quickly grow defensive, saying most families were in the same shape. "It was not *The Grapes of Wrath*," she'd emphasize, and she was right. We were not prosperous but neither were we poor. By carefully managing the family finances, Mother and Dad could provide what we needed, although there was little left over for indulgences until Red was sure he could get work.

Dad had been assured by the Corps of Engineers that he'd have a job and housing once the town they planned to build for the influx of workers began to take shape. In the meantime, he quickly found work with a private contractor building the road to the dam site.

But shelter was a big problem. Mother and Dad were relieved when they found two large rooms atop a white frame house in the tiny farm town of Ravinia, a bare-bones commercial center for the surrounding farmers. Ravinia was in the heart of the Yankton Indian reservation. It had a general store, a gas station, a tavern, and a redbrick school for grades one through twelve.

Our new accommodations were spare but comfortable. My brothers and I made bedrooms out of two large walk-in closets, where my parents also stored economy-size sacks of flour and sugar they were able to get for a good price. Mother and Dad had their own bedroom, and another large room was a combination living room, dining room, and kitchen. We had running water and a bathroom but no hot water, so a small two-burner gas stove was fired up almost constantly, heating pans of water for cooking, dishwashing, and bathing.

Our landlord lived on the first floor, where his frequent drunken tirades against his wife rose through the heating grates and disturbed our peace. Finally Mike, who showed a fearlessness at age three that served him well when he later served as a Marine in Vietnam, went to the porous grate and yelled, "Hey, shut up down there." It worked, for a while.

Most of our neighbors shared our working-class way of life. There were no lawyers, bankers, or doctors in town. The "uniform" of the men was overalls and a work shirt. Wives and mothers wore simple housedresses, generally with an apron tied in place. The general store was operated by a young Navy veteran, and on Sundays the block-long main street was packed with the cars of farmers who had attended early mass and then stopped off at a local tavern for a neighborly glass of beer.

Although I was only seven, my parents had no fear of letting me ride my bike around town or the short distance out to a friend's farm. The entire community was an extended day-care center. Although our stay was brief, I have vivid memories of the tomboy neighbor who taught me to ride a bike; another neighbor who introduced me to basketball, which has remained a lifelong passion; the farm-kid class-mate who invited me out to the country for a sleepover and an introduction to the exotic world of milking cows, threshing, and picking corn by hand.

For others in the village, life was not as pleasant. A very poor family lived in a one-room garage behind our rooming house. The children were shoeless most of the time, and their clothing was little more than rags. The father supplemented the family's meager diet with deer meat poached from a nearby Sioux reservation. If they received any help from the county or local charities, it wasn't evident in their wardrobe or lifestyle.

Two brothers who lived on a farm at the edge of town were hopeless drunks and the object of juvenile cruelties. We'd mock and mimic their stumbling gait or douse them with water as they were trying to sleep off a big drunk on the bench in front of the tavern. No one seemed to care or tried to intervene.

Ravinia was a snapshot of America in transition from the party-line telephone system to rotary dial; from kerosene lamps to full electrical power; from pre–WWII cars with push-button starters and manual shifts to automobiles with a fluid drive and good heaters. Jim and Ethel bought one of the first postwar Pontiacs, a long, roomy automobile with a prominent hood ornament of an Indian chief. It was their first new car since they'd lost the farm fourteen years earlier, and it was also the last car they owned; in their later years, Mother and Dad provided their transportation.

We stayed in Ravinia only six months, moving to the new town hastily erected by the Corps of Engineers hard by the dam site. It was called Pickstown, after the Army general in charge of the project. When we arrived in midwinter of 1948, the town was still a work in progress, but our house was ready for occupancy at 111 Lewis, a paved street named for Meriwether Lewis.

It was a prefabricated three-bedroom duplex with a modern kitchen, bathroom, and utility room. The rooms were modest in size, but 111 Lewis was easily the most commodious home in which my parents had ever lived. The gas-fired cooking and heating appliances were a marvel to people who had spent a lifetime shoveling coal into furnaces or feeding kindling into wood-burning stoves. We had hot running water and a four-digit telephone number.

Most of the houses in the new town, small but fully modern duplexes and triplexes, were still under construction when we arrived. But seemingly overnight the community was complete, what a writer would later call a "shake-and-bake town." We had a large movie theater, a hospital, an interdenominational chapel, a

Pickstown and the Fort Randall Dam in 1955. The school was on the far side of the traffic oval.

Construction on the dam involved some of the largest earth-moving equipment ever built. My grandfather Jim Conley directed these trucks where to dump their loads.

hotel, a shopping center, a bowling alley, and a modern two-story school building. Although it stood in the remote reaches of South Dakota, far from any population center, Pickstown resembled the new suburban communities growing up around metropolitan areas to accommodate the baby boom following the war.

We shared a driveway with another duplex, occupied by the owners of Western Construction, the primary contractors on the first phase of the dam. The company was owned by the Everest family of Sioux City, Iowa, and their eldest son, Garland, was the on-site boss for the family. He left early and arrived home late, rarely pausing for small talk. We had never lived that close to such authority and wealth before, and I was always a little intimidated by his brusque presence. I was startled, then, to learn many years later that Garland was just thirty-four years old at the time.

Our first neighbors on the other side of our duplex were country people from southern Illinois. The father was a carpenter and the mother opened a beauty shop for women, but the family's real passion was country-and-western music: it drifted through our common

The Fort Randall Dam at completion. My friend Sylvan Highrock's house was covered by the lake.

The remnants of the chapel at the nineteenth-century Fort Randall, on the Missouri River. Sitting Bull was a prisoner of the 7th Cavalry at Fort Randall for a time.

wall most days and nights. Eddy Arnold singing "Cattle Call" and Vaughn Monroe's big hit, "Riders in the Sky," seemed to be welded to their phonograph turntable.

At first, Mother was irritated by the intrusion. She and Red were big-band aficionados—fans of the late Glenn Miller, Benny Goodman, and Tommy and Jimmy Dorsey. But before long we were won over and looked forward to the slightly filtered concerts from next door, featuring the big names out of Nashville and the swing rhythms of Bob Wills and his inimitable sidemen, the Texas Playboys.

For my parents, Pickstown represented a welcome security: a steady year-round paycheck, good benefits, low-cost but comfortable housing, and a vibrant community of like-minded families from all across America. Daily life revolved around work, family, school, church, community.

Even now, fifty years later, when I encounter friends from those halcyon days, they say, "That was the best place we ever lived." A steady flow of new workers for different phases of the dam kept the population from ever growing stale. Although it didn't register with me at the time, I now realize that the families who moved into Pickstown were probably in awe of their surroundings. Everything was so new, the paint hardly seemed to be dry. Our very modern town and facilities generated a community pride, and the Army Corps of Engineers had a sizable maintenance and service staff to keep everything humming. New homes with new appliances stood in freshly planted lawns bordering newly laid sidewalks and newly paved streets. The school had the largest maplewood basketball court in the county, to go along with its new desks, new textbooks, and complete chemistry and biology laboratories. Pickstown was too remote to receive a television signal, so we were sealed off from that newly developing world. It was like living in a fifties biosphere.

It was an exciting time for an adventurous and inquisitive young boy. I began the second semester of second grade with a handful of other students in a cramped classroom that had been squeezed into another duplex on the edge of a wild stretch of hills, creeks, and bluffs along the Missouri River. Rattlesnakes were not uncommon on our playground, although no one was bitten. We were all young immigrants to this new land, the sons and daughters of civil engineers, geologists, heavy-equipment operators, laborers, bureaucrats, welders, and mechanics.

The prairie around Pickstown was mostly treeless, so the Corps surrounded the town with what it called shelter belts, thick rows of trees to break the merciless north wind that blew across the winter prairie. To help shade our kitchen, my father and a few friends found a young American elm out in the country and dug it up to be transplanted in our backyard. They had to trim the roots with their sharp jackknives to make it fit, and my mother watched skeptically, saying, "I'll eat my hat if that tree grows."

It thrived. And so did the grassy lawns and bountiful vegetable and flower gardens that complemented the neat rows of houses lining the graceful spokes of wide, paved streets connecting the community. Few families stayed in Pickstown much longer than two or three years; as the dam progressed, new contractors came, bringing in a new workforce. The old workers then moved on. Yet, however long they planned to stay, most families spent long spring and summer hours outside, planting, trimming, mowing, and decorating as if they were going to be there forever.

There was a community-wide fixation on neatness and orderliness that began with the Corps of Engineers' military discipline and extended to the most modest homes, little more than cabins, that were rented by the laborers, truck drivers, and other more transient employees. The refrain "Cleanliness is next to godliness" was a holy watchword beyond the lawns and gardens. Cars were washed and waxed, to be placed in garages where mechanical and carpenter's tools were stored with military precision. A woman could be attractive, a loving wife, and an attentive mother, but if she was an indifferent housekeeper that's how she would be known.

Pickstown's modern chapel had a rotating altar to serve Protestants, Catholics, and Jews, although only the Protestants actually worshiped there. Catholics worshiped at a church in a nearby town, and if there were any Jewish families, they'd have had to drive to Sioux City, Iowa, more than a hundred miles away, to find a synagogue. On our family tree we were the Protestant branch—an anomaly given the Catholic roots on both sides.

We were generic Protestants as an outgrowth of my mother's childhood in the Methodist church. Her grandfather Conley had left Roman Catholicism, apparently because of an unhappy experience as an altar boy. My father's mother was a Catholic and raised most of her children in that faith, but by the time my father came along, the last of ten, his attendance at mass was somehow overlooked: one more manifestation of his go-it-alone childhood. When Dad married Mother, he followed her into Protestant churches on their road-crew circuit of the Midwest, so by the time we arrived in Pickstown, this branch of the Brokaws was clearly back in the traditions of its Huguenot heritage.

Regular attendance at church and Sunday school was a fixed rhythm of my young life. It was an uncomplicated, ecumenical experience; we worshiped with Southern Baptists, Scandinavian Lutherans, and Midwestern Methodists, all led by an enthusiastic and athletic young Congregational minister, Robert Grimm, and his equally winning wife, Bobbie.

Reverend Grimm, a tall, handsome man with a toothy smile and jet-black hair to match his robes, led us through services that were mainstream Christianity with a decided emphasis on joy and positive thinking, light on guilt or complicated ritual. We took communion in our pews, drinking from small vials of grape juice, and the host was Wonder bread cut into small cubes.

Sin was not a complex subject. The Ten Commandments summed it up, and the only one of those I personally had any experience with was Thou Shalt Not Steal. Stealing, even petty theft, was a grave sin in my boyhood; to this day, I can cite the names of the perpetually light-fingered, including the choirboy who regularly pilfered girlie magazines from the drugstore. I suppose I may have pocketed a few penny bubblegum pieces, but the prospect of getting caught and facing the disapproval of the community and the wrath of my father was a powerful deterrent.

As for Thou Shalt Not Take the Lord's Name in Vain, I guess I figured my dad and his fellow workers had an exemption, for they were constantly but benignly profane. If I had known the word then, I would have said, "Lord, profanity is their patois; they can't work without it." My father never used swear words in social settings and never failed to use them at work. They were all-purpose verbs, nouns, and hyphens, as in "These windshield goddamn wipers need to be replaced."

I attended an all-boys Sunday school class and memorized the names of the books of the Bible without spending much time on their content, except for a few select passages such as the Twenty-third Psalm. Our teacher would reward a particularly responsive class with a swimming trip to the Missouri, where we dove into the swift current off an uprooted cottonwood tree snagged in the sand, surfacing just in time to catch the tail end of the exposed roots.

Ours was the quintessential white-bread Christian community. I knew no Jews or, for that matter, outspoken unbelievers. Most of the local Indians worshiped in their own country churches—either Episcopal or Roman Catholic, owing to the work of nineteenth-century missionaries. When it came to faith, the only real diversity was between Rome and Luther. Church and Christianity were fixed values, along with work and family, but they were not badges to be displayed prominently, much less defiantly, as they are in so many circles today.

Church suppers and summer picnics were part of the ecumenical experience, because the many regions represented by the workforce took us well beyond the usual fried chicken, potato salad, and Jell-O. Brandy Fitzhugh and his wife, who had grown up in the South, introduced us to hush puppies. We were told the dish was invented by raccoon hunters in the back country who wanted to quiet their dogs around the campfire. They'd fry up a piece of dough and toss it to the dogs, saying "Hush, puppy." Families from Missouri and Mississippi brought bowls of okra, butter beans, and collard greens. Some of my friends from the South had a taste for fried squirrel. My mother drew the line at that culinary adventure.

But Monday through Friday, with time-and-a-half pay for Saturday, work was the fundamental religion of the community. I knew the work shifts of all my playmates' fathers. If a dad was working "graveyard," midnight to eight A.M., you rarely visited during the day for fear of disturbing his sleep. Swing shift was four P.M. to midnight, and in those households you'd often find the father eating supper at two in the afternoon.

The good wages were an object of constant attention: who was making how much in overtime that week and how they would be spending it; what skills at the dam paid the most per hour and how to get one of those jobs; who was managing money well and who was just showing off. Despite the new working-class prosperity, old habits died hard. After cleanliness, frugality was next closest to godliness. The mother of one of my boyhood friends made him wear unmatched socks for Saturday play. No sense in throwing out a sock just because its mate has a hole.

Every family seemed to make room in their budgets for one nonessential item: cigarettes. Almost every shirt pocket and purse contained a pack of smokes; they were a ubiquitous part of life at work and home. A good Zippo lighter was treated like a fine tool. It was cleaned and refueled at regular intervals so it wouldn't fail the nicotine-addicted owner at a critical moment. Large ashtrays and table lighters were prominently displayed in every living room.

Smokers were also known by their brands. Dad smoked Camels, unfiltered and powerful. Others were hooked on Lucky Strikes, which featured a physician in one of their magazine advertisements. Big tobacco was a masterful marketer of images well before the Marlboro Man. The makers of Pall Mall, an extra long cigarette, claimed the length "travels the smoke further . . . and makes it *mild.*" L&M cigarettes were "just what the doctor ordered."

In 1954, two epidemiologists reported the

results of a two-year study on the dangers of smoking, and the results were startling: men who smoked had a much higher rate of coronary heart disease and several forms of cancer, especially lung cancer. Still, ten years passed before the U.S. Surgeon General issued a national alert officially linking smoking to heart disease and cancer.

But in my boyhood, cigarette smoking was as much a part of everyday life as breathing and eating. Out on the windy prairie, smokers automatically held their cigarettes between index finger and thumb, tucking the lit end into a protective cup formed by their hand.

To save money, Dad would sometimes revert to "roll your own" cigarettes. He'd carry in his overalls a can of Prince Albert tobacco and those little folders of cigarette papers, but before long he would return to the Camels he so loved. Smoking, I discovered, was not a genetic trait. Dad started when he was ten and didn't stop until his mid-fifties. I sneaked a pack of his Camels when I was about twelve and nearly expired after lighting up half the pack. After high school I started again, but it was never enjoyable, and so I gave it up in my late twenties.

Just as men were known by their cigarette brands, families were known by their cars as much as by the father's occupation, their religion, or the number of their children. The standard was either a Ford or Chevrolet; any other model was sure to cause comment. The town doctor, kindly Edmund Flynn, ordered a Cadillac one year and took a ribbing about it every day. Other models from that time when the American auto industry ruled the world have come and gone: the Hudson; the Henry J., the first compact; the Nash, with seats that folded all the way back, the car teenage lovers coveted.

In 1950, Dad, who had always been a Ford man, switched to Chevrolet. My parents' first new car, in keeping with their utilitarian ways, was a bottom-of-the-line battleship-gray sedan with a standard shift and no radio. At that point in their lives—and for several years after—it was the largest single purchase of their marriage: a little more than $1,700, and they paid cash. It was the Brokaw family transportation for the next ten years, the car in which Bill and Mike and I learned to drive, and the car all of us used for our first dates.

Until we had the new car, most vacations

consisted of weekend trips to the Black Hills of South Dakota, where we picnicked beneath the transformed granite outcropping called Mount Rushmore. Or we drove back to Bristol for family reunions. But in the summer of 1950, Mother and Dad decided on the working-class version of the Grand Tour. We set off to see Dad's brother Richard and his family in a suburb of Long Beach, California. Two weeks and three thousand miles round-trip. Bill and Mike and I occupied the backseat, where Red had built a plywood insert to fit the foot well so we had a platform on which to stretch out, wrestle, nap, read, and play with time-killing toys.

Bill, the middle brother, was shy but mischievous, and Mike, the youngest, was happy-go-lucky but always ready to roughhouse—a volatile combination. Bill and Mike liked to gang up on me, in a good-natured fashion. They had reason to team up, since as the oldest I had a room of my own, while they were forced to share. As the oldest, I also got the first bike, the first BB gun, and the first fishing rod. It wasn't fair, but birth order is one of life's lotteries. Also, I realize in retrospect, I invoked my seniority when it was to my advantage, which understandably irritated them, and so we often wound up in a backseat scrum.

Mother and Dad had saved $500 in those pre-credit-card days, and they managed their vacation money well. We drove across Wyoming, staying with friends from the Igloo days, and then into Salt Lake City for a tour of the Mormon Tabernacle before pushing on hard for Las Vegas, where I slipped a quarter into a slot machine and got $2.50 back. The coffee-shop owner rushed over to say I was well below the legal playing limit, but he let me keep my bonanza.

We stopped at Boulder Dam much as a geologist's family might stop at the Grand Canyon. We felt connected to big construction projects across wild rivers, a connection I later came to question when I realized that the dam-everything mentality of the fifties had serious environmental consequences.

Driving into California was the Brokaw family equivalent of Dorothy entering Oz: we knew we weren't in South Dakota anymore. Ocean surf and palm trees; avocados, and strawberries as large as apricots; television, which had not yet reached our corner of the Great Plains; a side trip to Tijuana, where I spent a quarter for a sombrero with my name painted on it.

I accompanied my mother and father on a

package tour of the Los Angeles sights we'd heard about: Hollywood and Vine, the Griffith Park Observatory, the popular daytime television show *Queen for a Day,* the Farmers Market.

It was the beginning of my realization that there was a wider world beyond my native provinces, and possibilities for my ambitions were just then beginning to take shape. They were not really formed, beyond a taste for adventure and prosperity, both of which had modest proportions in a ten-year-old's fantasy. Mother and Dad were already saving for a college education for their three boys, and this trip was part of learning to take the first step beyond our door.

We drove up the coast to San Francisco, where a family joke was born. Mother had the impression that cable cars resembled funiculars, not the trolleys she'd known in Minneapolis. So when a trolley stopped in front of the St. Francis Hotel, she asked where we could find a cable car to ride. The tourist-weary conductor looked at her and said, "Lady, this is as close as you're gonna get. This *is* a cable car."

San Francisco was a memorable stop. When Mother took me to buy a new pair of shoes at J. C. Penney, we were approached by a dapper little man in a bow tie. He said, "Do you know who I am?" Mother said, "Yes. You're J. C. Penney, I just read your life story in the Minneapolis paper." "Good deal," I thought. "J. C. Penney! He's bound to give me a new pair of shoes." Instead, he turned, snapped his fingers at a clerk, and said, "Come help these people. They want to buy this boy some shoes."

I couldn't wait to get back to South Dakota to tell my friends I had met the biggest celebrity of my life. It was also a foretaste of what a friend later called "Brokaw's lucky star." Wherever I went, something interesting or memorable almost always happened.

We returned home via the Sierra Nevada mountains, Yellowstone Park, and the familiar Black Hills. When I got back to Pickstown I might as well have been Richard Halliburton. I had tales of faraway places for my pals, most of whom had never seen the ocean or a city larger than Minneapolis. Later, when I worked as a reporter in California, I never tired of its allure, in part, I think, because I was seduced at such an early and impressionable age.

But then Pickstown was no ordinary small town in a remote location. The combination of the round-the-clock construction on the

dam, which could be viewed from several vantage points on nearby bluffs, and the unique
layout of the new town, seemingly just out of
the box, drew a steady stream of visitors. Farm
families and residents of other small towns in
Nebraska and Iowa as well as South Dakota
would drive the new paved roads in wonder,
taking in the large bowling alley and rec center, the largest movie theater in five counties,
the new school that faced a graceful traffic
oval, the lively soda fountain and gleaming
hospital. We felt superior, whether we were
justified or not.

Since Pickstown was a community with no
history of its own, some families with a difficult
past were happy to arrive and get a fresh start,
or at least put their troubles on hold during the
run of prosperity. There was such a concentra-
tion on the job at hand and on the new hopes
for better times after the Depression and world
war, few had much interest in earlier difficulties, but occasionally a hint would emerge. The
mother of one friend had several children with
different last names, and her relationship with
her current husband was problematic. One day
while buying stamps at the post office, she
shared her escape plan with my mother: She

carried with her at all times eight hundred-dollar bills, hidden in her billfold, just in case she awoke one morning to find her husband gone. In those pre-inflationary days, $800 was enough to finance a fresh start. That story, from my mother over supper one night when I was about twelve, was startling. I idolized my friend, a slightly older boy who was a gifted athlete and unerringly polite. He lived in a trailer with his parents and several siblings, so I knew that his home was physically crowded, but until I heard the story of the hundred-dollar bills I did not fully appreciate the difference between his family life and my own.

Like the tourists, Pickstown residents found the dam-building fascinating. It was not unusual for families to drive to a vantage point above the river after supper and look down on the sprawl of construction and mighty earth-moving machines, working beneath bright lights, to rearrange the ancient landscape of chalkstone bluffs and bottomland. The dump trucks had tires so large they dwarfed a man standing next to them. Cutting machines ate away at the tightly packed chalkstone. Enormous electricity-powered shovels with buckets large enough to hold a sedan chewed away at the riverbanks like mutant beavers.

The Missouri River was first slowed, then redirected, and finally backed up behind the intake tunnels, powerhouse, and 166-foot-high berm when closure was accomplished in 1953. President Eisenhower flipped a switch in the Oval Office to activate the eight turbines that, when powered by the focused force of the water, would transmit electricity to seven states.

Life magazine and regional newspapers such as *The Des Moines Register* did extensive features on the Missouri River development and I remember the pride we felt at being part of something important enough to be noticed beyond our provincial borders. South Dakota was so sparsely populated and so remote that I searched for any sign that the rest of the world knew who we were and what we were doing with our lives. If a magazine advertisement listed the branch offices of a company and none were in South Dakota, I felt let down somehow.

News from the outside came via radio and two in-state daily newspapers, the Mitchell *Daily Republic* and the Yankton *Press & Dako-*

tan. The Sunday edition of *The Minneapolis Tribune* was also available. I delivered them all. My territory covered the north end of town, home to probably three hundred families, and yet I remember that only thirty-five or forty subscribed to a newspaper, for whatever reason. Most, I suspect, got what news they felt they needed from the evening and nighttime radio newscasts, local and network, or from the glimpses of national and international events that made it to the Movietone newsreels at the local movie theater.

Without television, we were denied the front-row seats to history available to our city brethren. For example, the Army-McCarthy hearings, in which the infamous Senator Joe McCarthy, the swarthy Republican from Wisconsin, attempted to smear U.S. Army workers as Communists, appeared only in the newsreels before the feature films. The historic 1954 U.S. Supreme Court decision *Brown v. Board of Education,* ending legal school segregation in America, barely made a ripple in our largely sealed-off existence.

The Minneapolis Tribune will always be one of my favorite newspapers, for it gave me my first opportunity for adventure travel. The paper offered a free trip to Minneapolis and tickets to a University of Minnesota football game to any carrier who signed up a certain number of new customers. Since Pickstown had a constantly evolving workforce, I had a ready pool of new prospects and I almost always nailed the prize.

One year, when I was just twelve, I had signed up enough customers to take my friend Jimmy Brown with me. We took a bus a hundred miles to Sioux City, where we boarded an all-night local train to Minneapolis, stopping often in the autumnal darkness to pick up freight, farm products, even a casket filled with the remains of some anonymous Minnesotan. Jimmy and I slept not a wink as the conductor kept us entertained with tales of railroading and tours of the crew's sleeping quarters. These were cozily familiar to the offspring of workingmen, with their thermos bottles of coffee, wall calendars, and thick wool mackinaw coats that hung from hooks above the simple cots, swaying gently with the train's rolling motion.

Arriving at the Milwaukee Road depot in Minneapolis at dawn was thrilling for this small-town boy with big-city aspirations buried somewhere in his adolescent consciousness. It was a cold morning and the locomotives belched great clouds of steam onto the platform, where we were met by the *Tribune* representative.

Memorial Stadium, the home of the University of Minnesota Golden Gophers, was filled to capacity for the game against the University of Illinois. I knew every Gopher player from a religious weekly reading of the *Tribune* sports section, which was printed on paper colored a light rose and generally known as "the Peach." My hero was Minnesota's All-America halfback, Paul Giel, and when he ran past our end-zone seats and into the locker room at the end of a winning game, I thought that was as close as I would ever get to greatness.

However, later that same day Jimmy and I decided to see if on our own we could get tickets to see the Minneapolis Lakers and the Harlem Globetrotters play in the old Minneapolis auditorium. We managed to get seats in the nosebleed section for, as I recall, twenty-five cents, but there was a bonus. As we explored the corridors before the game, we came upon the Lakers' great center, George Mikan, chatting with some fans in the hallway. We boldly introduced ourselves as basketball players on the junior high team back in Pickstown. Mikan, who had been voted the best basketball player of the half-century, was cordial and encouraging.

Many years later I was able to recount this story when I introduced Mikan at an annual dinner for the onetime All Stars of the NBA. It was in a room filled with other basketball greats who had become personal friends, including Bill Russell, John Havlicek, Bill Bradley, and Dave DeBusschere, and I almost felt like that crewcut twelve-year-old, Tommy Brokaw, looking up, wondering how in hell I got here.

That early Minneapolis trip is reflective of more innocent times, but it's also a commentary on what I was *not* seeing as an impressionable child from the hinterland. I loved the pace and excitement of downtown Minneapolis, the brightly lit restaurants open well into the night; the Nankin, a venerable Chinese restaurant in downtown Minneapolis with inlaid mother-of-pearl on the dining tables; Dayton's, the large, elegant department store, whose wares bore no resemblance to the pedestrian offerings of Pickstown merchants. I felt every inch a country boy as I looked with awe on the honey-haired coeds in camel's-hair coats festooned with mums, waving pom-poms at the football game, the Gophers in their maroon and gold uniforms and the Lakers in an arena that could have held the entire population of Pickstown.

My young life was largely defined by the parameters of the white working-class culture in which I was being raised, in the unique small town with the short life span. By the summer of 1955 it was clear that the best years of Pickstown were already past. The population had dropped precipitously with the completion of major work on the dam. But in the time we had lived there, from the second semester of the second grade through my freshman year in high school, I had formed lifelong friendships and interests, especially in the allure of the primal qualities of the Missouri River and the landscape it had carved over millions of years.

CHAPTER 4

Talk

IF MOVING MACHINERY IS A SYMBOL OF my father's life, I suppose a microphone is the tool with which I am most associated. For as long as I or anyone in my family can remember, I have been a chatterbox, someone with a verbal facility and an eager attitude about exercising it. In the culture in which I was raised, that was a curious trait; most of the inhabitants were strong silent types, people who let their work speak for them. I suppose I got rather used to having the floor, because no one else much wanted it.

I always attribute my verbosity to my mother's Irish ancestry, although, in fact, I remember her father as a shy, reserved man, more inclined to reading than speaking. My

grandmother Ethel was a lively conversational-
ist, and so is my mother. Apparently they are
the source of this inclination to let no word go
unspoken, for certainly it was much more the
product of nature than of nurture.

In my mind's eye, I can still see my first public performance. It was in a large hall crowded
with men in uniform and the civilians who
performed the nonmilitary tasks at Igloo. It
was Christmas, 1944; I was just four years old,
and I had been chosen to open the holiday
pageant.

Although the scene remains quite vivid in
my memory—the smoke from hundreds of lit
cigarettes forming a blue haze over the pro-
ceedings, the wooden folding chairs, and the
ropes of tinsel looping along the walls—alas, I
can remember only the opening line of my
welcome to the crowd.

It began, "They said I was too young to
speak a piece tonight . . . ," but the rest is lost
in the black hole of more than half a century of
other impressions crowded onto the recollection cells. What I do remember is that I was
paid for my performance. My father stood at
the back of the hall and held up a silver dollar.
If he could hear my every word, he said, I

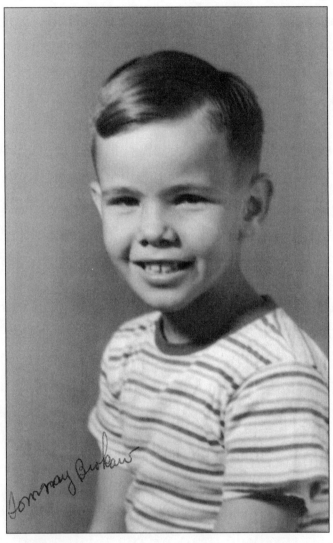

Tommy Brokaw in the first grade.

would get that silver dollar. It was an enormous sum for a four-year-old at a time when a nickel would buy a huge ice cream cone.

I just loved to talk, and I soon had an opinion on just about everything. Fortunately, my parents and my teachers indulged me. I was quick to raise a hand in class and, unlike most of my classmates, I wanted to be chosen to read aloud. By the time I reached second grade, my motor mouth was fully engaged. In Ravinia, named by the local Czech population for a city in their native land, my teacher was Frances Morrow, a handsome red-haired woman who lived with her husband and two teenage daughters on a tidy farm just north of town.

Frances was a seminal figure in my life. She encouraged me to read above my grade level and listened patiently to my commentary on whatever happened to be going on in my family, on Main Street, in the other grades, anywhere. She also played along with my rich imagination.

Once, when she developed laryngitis and had to limit her speaking, I was so intrigued that the next day I arrived with my own mock case and told her in a fake husky voice that I couldn't speak. She gravely went along with my charade and expressed great astonishment at my rapid recovery the following day.

Her real contribution, however, was in her commitment to the fundamentals, especially reading and spelling. She was a strict advocate of phonics and spelling bees, wisely dividing the class so even the slower students could be on the winning team in a spell-down. She inspired and pushed along those of us who were eager to learn while never slighting others who were painfully shy or a beat behind on the reading curve. It was a teaching tour de force.

More than fifty years later, I returned to Ravinia to thank Frances for her attention and, most of all, for her commitment to the fundamentals of reading and language that have been so central to my life. Although she was a widow by then, and recently diagnosed with what turned out to be a fatal cancer, she was still a handsome woman.

We gathered her daughters, now grown and raising families in the area, and went to lunch in a nearby town, where we were joined by one of my second-grade classmates, a fetching blonde. She and I had borne the royal titles of prince and princess in a long-ago school carnival.

Frances had remained active in education, consulting on reading programs at a local college, and she had never given up on the old-fashioned phonics method or on spelling drills. When I said there seemed to be a slow return to that way of teaching reading, she replied, "I can't understand why they abandoned it. It worked so well."

After my family left Ravinia, midway through my second-grade year, I continued to talk my way through elementary school, prompting most of my teachers to note on my report cards something to the effect that "Tommy is doing well in all his subjects, but he does need to work harder at not talking so much in class when it's not his turn." For the most part, however, I was allowed to chatter on.

Two teachers, particularly, in addition to Frances Morrow, had a gift for directing my fascination with my own voice, and in a more concentrated form. Elaine Petersen, in the fifth grade, and Harlan Holmes, in the seventh, were two young educators steeped in the midwestern tradition of exacting standards in public schools. They introduced me to public declamation, a holdover from the days before radio and television, when the most accessible form of entertainment in the rural areas was public speaking. Since our area had no television signal, there remained an audience for live local performances, and I was readily available.

Mrs. Petersen and Mr. Holmes introduced me to Robert Benchley's witty essays on everyday life and to the evocative language of Lincoln's Gettysburg Address, Gray's "Elegy Written in a Country Churchyard," and Whitman's tragic "O Captain! My Captain!" as well as to other more pedestrian texts on a variety of subjects. I would memorize them and perform them just for my class or, often, at a nighttime school assembly to which townspeople were invited.

One winter, I was taking great theatrical liberties with a piece on a boy smoking cigars for the first time. In the audience was my grandfather Jim Conley, a sentimental Irishman who was capable of tearing up at the sound of the national anthem on the radio. As I began my hammy performance, I could hear my grandfather's throaty guffaws; by the middle of the piece, while I was staggering around overcome by the power of the mimed cigars, the entire audience was in an uproarious mood, laughing hard at the bravura of my performance. But

Grandpa was convulsed with sobs, weeping openly in pride at the audacity of his oldest grandchild.

My grandfather might have been proud and amused, but I am sure many of my friends and their families wondered if I would ever shut up. I especially liked hanging around the older kids, for they seemed so worldly, and for the most part they treated me as a kind of mascot. By the time I was fourteen, my best friend in Yankton was a smooth-talking North Carolinian by the name of Don Vaughn, who was three years older.

Don was handsome, athletic, and theatrical. He was popular for his locker-room mimicry of teachers, coaches, and other students and for his spot-on imitation of an Andy Griffith routine. But what impressed me most was that he wanted to have a career as a radio disc jockey. I couldn't imagine the audacity of someone from our tiny town thinking that he could actually get hired to work in radio.

Radio was our principal link to the rest of the world, since as late as 1955, when most of the country was lit up with the glow from television sets, we still had no TV signal. Radio was a powerful force from a distant place and

beyond my ability to imagine I might have a
place in it. After all, our large living room cabinet radio brought us the news of the world
through the voices of Edward R. Murrow and
Lowell Thomas. Though youngsters in more
settled areas were growing up with the
Mouseketeers, Kukla, Fran, and Ollie, and
Howdy Doody, I remained a child of radio,
hooked on the sound effects of the Lone
Ranger; a detective called the Fat Man; Jack
Benny; Fibber McGee and Molly; and Burns
and Allen.

The local news came from WNAX, a powerful CBS affiliate in Yankton, and I was a
devotee of a folksy newscaster by the name of
Whitey Larson who broadcast from a satellite
studio in Sioux City, Iowa, another fifty miles
down the Missouri from Yankton.

Larson's six o'clock and ten o'clock reports
always opened with the weather forecast—the
most critical news of the day on the Great
Plains, home to some of the most savage
weather in North America.

Whitey would often begin, "Well, it's going
to snow tomorrow, but it won't be the shoveling kind, so we should be okay," or "We're
gonna get some rain tomorrow, but, ladies, I

think you'll still be able to hang out the wash."
The rest of the day's news, from the latest on
the Korean War to scandals in Washington, was
delivered more straightforwardly, but Whitey's
down-home style always left me with the feeling he was sitting there in our small living
room, telling it just to us.

Later a friend told me that Whitey played in
the Sioux City municipal band and that on
concert nights he would broadcast the late
news while wearing his band uniform. I often
think of that when someone fusses over what I
should wear on the *NBC Nightly News*. "Hell,"
I think, "maybe I should just send off for one
of Whitey's old band uniforms."

CHAPTER 5

Games

FOR WHATEVER REASON, I'VE ALWAYS been hardwired for memory. I can see clearly in my mind's eye events from very early in my life. Not only can I see the events, but I remember my reaction to them as well. From an early age I was treated as a precocious child, and I quickly began to believe all the praise coming my way. It led me to think that whatever I chose to do, I would do well. So by the age of six or seven I had developed an acute consciousness of my determination to be front and center in whatever was going on, whether it was the school Christmas pageant or "pump, pump, pull away" during recess. I guess I thought I was a natural, whatever the calling.

At an early age I was drawn to athletics, the

games of the Midwest: summer baseball, autumn football, and winter basketball, with track and field as a spring diversion. In our small pool of grade-school athletes in Pickstown, I was always above average, even occasionally a star, but I began to notice that no matter how hard I practiced, some of my friends were progressing faster. Speed—or, more accurately, the lack of it—became a drawback I constantly had to manage by playing smarter, anticipating the next move so I could get an early jump on a ground ball or cut off a drive to the basket.

It might have been wise to recognize early on that there would be a limit to my athletic prowess and achievements and to concentrate instead on my more natural gifts. Once, I qualified for the state track meet as a pole vaulter. As I stepped off the bus, filled with pride but also certain I would be eliminated in the early rounds, a coach from my junior-high years looked at me with wry amusement and said, "Why are *you* here? To speak?" We both had a good laugh.

I stayed in the game, whatever the season. I couldn't resist the action or, I suppose, the chance to perform in front of a crowd. In every

I was a starting guard, but there was no reason to retire number 20!

LETTER WINNERS

The Yankton High School varsity basketball team my senior year, 1958. We finished with a disappointing loss the town has not forgotten.

BASKETBALL BUCKS OF 1958

sport I made lasting friendships or learned enduring lessons. Some of my favorite childhood memories revolve around sports. They were a leavening influence on my life, because I often had to accept a secondary status while in most of my other pursuits I was accustomed to being at the head of the parade.

Sports also gave me a life of vicarious thrills as I got to sit in ever larger grandstands, watching World Series games, Super Bowls, or NBA All-Star Games, sitting on the finish line in Olympic stadiums or just behind the royal box at Wimbledon. When I attend one of those big events, I always remember the thrill of playing in the much smaller venues of my youth. When the film *Hoosiers* was released in 1986, I was so enthralled I wrote an essay for *The New York Times* describing my long affair with basketball, my first passion. I recalled how, when I was eight years old and living with my family in those two large rooms on the second floor of that white frame house in Ravinia, one of my winter diversions was an imaginary basketball game played with a rolled-up sock lofted toward the space between the top of a door frame and the ceiling. Although that was almost forty years ago, I remember the inner

FOOTBALL LETTERMEN

As the backup quarterback I didn't play much, but I knew how to pose!

The varsity football team my senior year, 1958. We were conference champions—and I had a good view of all the games from the sidelines.

voice that guided me: "We're down to the final seconds of the South Dakota State 'B' basketball championship, everyone, and Brokaw has the ball, his team trailing by a point. The crowd is on its feet. You can't hear yourself think. Ten seconds. Brokaw moves to the top of the key! Five seconds! He gives a little head fake, jumps, shoots! It's *good!*"

The rolled-up sock went in every time. My teammates never failed to carry me off the floor. The little blond girl who coolly ignored my overtures during second-grade alphabet recital realized what a fool she had been. It was all I asked for in life. Alas, I never did win a state tournament; indeed, the one time I did appear, I managed to blow a layup, dribble off my foot, and, finally, suffer the ignominy of being benched for the semifinal because our uptight coach caught me in the middle of some off-limits horseplay back at the hotel.

That was my junior year. The following year I was much more composed and, having repaired my relationship with the coach, I was looking forward to a triumphant tournament. Then, disaster. We were upset in the qualifying round by a smaller town whose team was led by an aggressive guard named Joe Thorne. He was in my face all night long. My last chance to fulfill a life's dream—gone, less than a month after my eighteenth birthday. There isn't a year I don't recall that loss and the enormous hole it blew in my expectations.

Nonetheless, often when I take my seat at Madison Square Garden for a Knicks game, I think back to the small towns where shafts of filtered sunlight illuminated the well-worn wooden floor of the tiny gym; the bare-pipe, peeling-paint look of the basement locker room; the sweaty intensity of the players; the friends, family, and neighbors hovering in those close quarters; the boorish but loyal behavior of the Main Street businessmen.

In tiny Geddes, South Dakota, the gymnasium was also an auditorium. The playing floor, doubling as a stage, was elevated about four feet above the seating, so diving for a loose ball was a risky proposition. The gym also had a large skylight that leaked after a heavy snow. I remember Sylvan Highrock leading a fast break and sliding from midcourt to the foul line. The referee called him for traveling.

Sylvan was a Sioux Indian, the only one on our team, and every year he was an especially welcome presence when Pickstown played Marty Mission, an all-Indian school along the Missouri River. He'd calm us as we entered what was for us a foreboding environment: a small dark gymnasium encircled by a balcony, where the Marty rooters would stand and chant as they looked down onto the playing floor while their team ran up big scores as players with names like John Two Hearts and Charlie Lone Wolf hit shot after shot. Basketball was a year-round sport at Marty Mission, and the players owned a home-court advantage quite unlike any other. We didn't have a chance.

Basketball was also a game of rituals and uniforms. Never have I felt more omnipotent than when I pulled on matching shorts and jersey, all-white tennis shoes and fleecy warmups, tops, and bottoms as a starting guard for the Yankton Bucks. This was much more than throwing a rolled-up sock against a wall or playing h-o-r-s-e in someone's driveway.

The locker room door would swing open. The band would be playing the school fight song. The crowd would be on its feet, cheering as the cheerleaders called out our names: Whisler, Eide, Soulek, Pokorney, Brokaw. We'd swing into our warmup routines: layups, outside jumpers, offensive rebounding, now defense, all very serious with barely a flicker of acknowledgment for the crowd, maybe a glance at a girlfriend or a potential girlfriend. Then, the game. The unalloyed joy of a victory, well played, without glaring, dumb mistakes, or the weekend-long pain of a loss. Losses that brought on hard stares and no consoling words from Main Street merchants.

I can still remember games, shots that were good and shots that missed, teammates and opposing players, including Joe Thorne, that tenacious guard who kept me from the state tournament my senior year. Thorne went on to play football at South Dakota State College and won a commission in the Army ROTC. In Washington, his name is in one of those directories at the entrance to the Vietnam Veterans Memorial. Lieutenant Josef Lloyd Thorne was killed in Vietnam in April 1965, a few months short of his twenty-fifth birthday.

Football was a slightly different experience. I began playing six-man football on the rocky and uneven fields around Pickstown, where the small school population limited us to the smaller game. Six on a side was a game for the very speedy, and that left me at quarterback, a position in which you were not allowed to run until handing off the ball at least once. As a 135-pound freshman, I often found myself in games against heavily muscled eighteen-year-old farm boys who outweighed me by forty pounds. In one game our entire senior back-field was injured, so the coach sent me in with two other lightweight running backs. We were getting pounded by a hard-hitting team of stout German Americans, and when I called a play involving one of our small running backs he held the huddle together for a moment and said, only half in jest, "Before we go back to the line of scrimmage I'd like to have a moment of silent prayer—for me."

I moved on to the eleven-man game in Yankton, our next home downstream, a perennial schoolboy powerhouse in South Dakota football. One of my classmates, Bill Whisler, was one of the greatest quarterbacks the state ever produced. His talent made it easy for me to be his backup, and when we won two championships I was able to make a small claim on the titles—very small. However, that experience gave me another perspective when I was asked to give the keynote address at a Heisman Trophy dinner more than thirty years later. In a

New York ballroom filled with the greatest college football players of the last five decades, I described my own limited abilities, saying that the scouting report on my quarterbacking abilities probably read, "Slow, but he has a weak arm."

As a senior in high school, I told the audience, I was playing mop-up quarterback in the final moments of the next-to-the-last game of the season and I was looking for some way to get my name in the record books. I had just directed a touchdown drive against our under-manned opponents, and in the huddle I confided to Mongrel, our huge center, and Dirty Glennie, the All-State guard to his right, that I wanted to carry the ball for the extra point so I could get on the board. Mongrel and Dirty Glennie, who got his nickname because his uniform was always dirty from playing so hard, quickly agreed to make it happen.

I took the snap from center and prepared to bull my way through the opposing line, but Mongrel and Dirty Glennie had opened a hole wide enough to drive a truck through. My moment of glory consisted of practically walking across the goal line, unmolested.

I went on to tell the Heisman dinner audience that one of the reasons I always admired football was because it required so many skills on one team and in one game. Brute strength combined with blinding speed; one-on-one collisions that make possible intricate patterns of deception and advancement; the working class up front and the white-collar workers in the backfield; throwing and catching; punting and kicking.

Football, I reminded them, is also a leveling playing field. For obvious reasons, it is gender-specific, but it is color-blind and pedigree-neutral. How much money your father has or how famous your mother's family may be is of no use once you put on the pads, cleats, and helmet. Then the question is: Can you block and tackle, run and throw, catch or kick?

At whatever level the game is played, football also creates lasting bonds. Many years after I left Yankton I returned to help console my mother after the death of my father. It was a warm early-summer morning, and I decided to go for a long run along a country road north of town.

As I loped along I could see a car turning out of a farm driveway about a mile away. I thought of Dirty Glennie and how he'd given me that one moment of glory. I knew he had returned to the family place after playing football at a local college. The car skidded to a stop beside me, and sure enough, Dirty Glennie tumbled out. "What the hell are you doing, running in this heat?" he asked, laughing. I pointed to his sizable middle and kidded him about his weight. And then we fell into an awkward silence, separated as we were now by so many years and such different lives.

Then Dirty Glennie did something I'll never forget. He raised his big, beefy forearm and said, "Hey, Brokes, if you ever need me, I could still clear them out for you." I laughed and told him I'd keep that in mind. As I turned to continue my morning run between the fields of corn and soybeans, I was misty with the sentiments of a time gone by.

Baseball was the summer game in every small town across the Midwest. Pickstown quickly assembled a formidable team from the country-boy construction workers. A lanky and canny pitcher, Vance Cobble, had made it all the way to Kansas City in the old American Association before straining his arm, but it was still stronger than the local competition, so for one magical summer we had the local equivalent of the Yankees.

I still remember many of the names— DeMarco at third, Eck at first, Mueller at shortstop, Cobble on the mound. They were my local heroes to go with Jackie Robinson, my idol on the faraway Brooklyn Dodgers. At the end of a workday they'd change into hot wool uniforms; the lights would go on at the ball park, with its all-dirt infield and rows of cars parked along the foul lines. Every competitive kid in town would take up a position across the street, behind home plate. There we chased foul balls and returned them for a dime apiece to Lowell Tiezen, the representative of the American Legion post that sponsored the team. When a new kid showed up in town, chasing fouls was his first try-out for speed and hustle.

I remember to this day seeing a new boy— someone said he was Bobby Gene Davenport from Muskogee, Oklahoma—who was as quick as a water bug, squirting after the errant balls. Bobby Gene grew up to be one the town's best athletes, a letterman and star in three sports. I could have predicted that the first summer night he cashed in all those foul balls he ran down.

Mornings, after mowing a lawn or two, I met my pals for our own game on the same ball field.

I have commented before that as a baseball fan I've been present at some magic moments— as a seventeen-year-old visiting New York from South Dakota, I managed to find my way to Ebbetts Field, home of my beloved Dodgers; in the press box at Dodger Stadium in Los Angeles on nights when Koufax was throwing, I'd wonder, "How does *anyone* hit that guy?"; I'd catch my home-state friend Dick Green, the second baseman for those championship Athletics teams of the seventies. I visited a Yankee locker room with Mantle and Maris, and sat with my family behind the Yankee dugout the night Reggie Jackson hit three home runs in a row off first pitches in a deciding game of the World Series against the Dodgers. My kids discarded their Dodger heritage on the spot and became Yankee fans.

Later I was in Dodger Stadium the night Kirk Gibson limped to the plate against Dennis Eckersley of the A's in the World Series and hit the most electrifying home run I will ever see. I got to know Joe DiMaggio, and Ted Williams sent me an autographed picture for Christmas a few years back. As a reporter I traveled with Hank Aaron for a month the summer before he hit home run 715.

But for all that, I cherish most the memories of two summers in the mid-fifties in Pickstown.

With other eleven- and twelve-year-old boys who were athletic and competitive, we formed two teams: the Pheasants (my team) and the Warriors. We organized bake sales and mowed lawns to raise money for sweatshirts and caps: red for the Pheasants, blue for the Warriors.

Baseball was the defining competition. We played every day during the summer on the town field. We had no umpires or adult supervision but we managed to get along surprisingly well, arriving at balls and strikes and outs by consensus. When there was an irreconcilable dispute, we often turned to the only non-player in our crowd, Johnny Strutz, a quiet and studious only child. He was always fair, and we accepted his rulings.

I can still remember the players: Chuck Gremmels, the chief Warrior, with his blistering fastball; Marc Rhoades, his best friend, behind the plate; my pal Jimmy Brown, a tough little catcher and daring base runner. I played shortstop and second base, like my hero, Jackie Robinson, and swung his signature bottle-handled bat.

From time to time we'd arrange games with nearby towns, persuading our mothers to drive us. The opposition would be surprised when we showed up without an adult manager, but our two captains would have settled on an all-star lineup and we'd take the field. Somehow it worked.

In those hot South Dakota summers the games were almost always in the mornings so we could reserve the afternoons for swimming in the nearby river or at a pool seven miles away. We'd wind up the day at the drugstore, teasing the high school girls who served us fountain Cokes and double-dip ice cream cones for a dime.

I have gone back a few times to drive the deserted road past the overgrown field that was our main ballpark, and another patch of prairie grass that was a place where the Pheasants and the Warriors often practiced in our red and blue sweatshirts and caps.

We assembled there in the second summer, each team lined up solemnly along the first and third baseline, our caps off. The preceding winter our friend Johnny Strutz, the quiet and fair arbiter, had died of leukemia. His house was just across the street, and Chuck Gremmels had gathered us to declare, "This will be known as Strutz Field—forever."

I learned a lot about baseball, friendship, and life during those summers with the Pheasants and the Warriors.

To this day, whatever else I have accomplished in life, when I return to South Dakota someone is sure to bring up a game in which I played, some success or a failure at an athletic event. Forty years later, at a reunion of Pickstown students, one of my slightly older friends, who had been an active athlete, wasn't much interested in my New York life or my career as a journalist. What he really wanted to know was how I fared in basketball when I moved to Yankton with its much larger high school. When I told him I was a starting guard my senior year, he was duly impressed.

To be sure, athletics is often overemphasized in small-town America. I've met several South Dakotans who have achieved great success in business, academics, or politics but, because they were not schoolboy athletes, still feel that their hometown peers never fully appreciated their gifts. It is a hard fact of life that even someone who dies a drunk and deadbeat is celebrated if he was a star of any high school team.

While I find that intellectually indefensible, I cannot emotionally separate myself from those long-ago moments under the lights of a ballpark or in the din of a small gymnasium or the camaraderie of a locker room. They taught me the lessons that come with teamwork, competition, winning and losing.

Two of my favorite coaches—Rich Greeno, who later became the national high school track coach of the year, and his friend, Don Baker—were just a few years older than I and so they were more like big brothers than authority figures. On long road trips Don and I would stand at the front of the bus and have a spirited competition over who knew more people in each town we passed through. Rich was the arbiter.

Once Don and I were both stumped by a small, fading village on a remote road. Suddenly, he shouted, "I know a man who bought a dog here once!" I turned to Rich, trusting his integrity, and he laughingly rejected Don's claim.

In 1996, when NBC was telecasting the Olympic Games in Atlanta, I was asked to speak at a dinner for past gold-medal winners. I invited Rich and his wife to be my guests and I arranged tickets for them at the opening ceremonies. I explained to the assembled atheletes at the dinner that I could never get to the gold medal stand when I was competing for Rich, but at least I got him to the dinner.

Rich and I both wished Don could have been along. Tragically, he died of a massive coronary in his mid-thirties, when he was coaching basketball at the University of South Dakota. I still think of him when I pass through small South Dakota towns, wondering if he knew any more "man bought a dog" stories.

When I was a senior in high school and getting discouraged about a long season as a backup quarterback to our star, I went to the coach, Don Allen, and said I thought I should quit. Allen, who had been a star college athlete and was a combat veteran of World War II, heard me out and then said, gently, "Well, Tom, I understand your frustration. You're used to being number one—the president of the student body, Boys State governor, you have the lead in the play. But what if all the students who didn't have those titles decided to quit? Where would we be?"

I went back to the locker room the next day and suited up, still frustrated but with a little more perspective. Coach Allen's only game-time concession was to have me loosen up on the sidelines a little earlier, as if he were thinking of sending me in. He knew and I knew that it was mostly a charade, but he'd given me an enduring lesson in the game beyond the goal lines and sidelines.

CHAPTER 6

Boys' Life

At what age do you begin to realize your limits? For me, the first dawning came when I was about seven or eight and I was asked to help form a children's chorus for Sunday school. Since I was the chattiest kid in the class, and a gregarious take-charge type, I suppose my teachers assumed I could sing. So did I, until I opened my mouth and began. Whatever it was that came out, it wasn't music. I could hear the musical scales, the pitch, the tone, but I was physically incapable of recreating them. Shortly, I was asked merely to stand in the chorus and leave the singing to others. I was surprised. It was my first real encounter with failure and I had no control over it.

My short and futile effort
to become a trombrone player.

Nonetheless, I was determined to press on. Mother and I persuaded my skeptical father to buy me a used trombone for $90. I wanted to emulate a bandleader named Buddy Morrow who had a popular number called "One Mint Julep" featuring some long trombone riffs. I joined a beginning instruments class with a few of my friends, who quickly progressed past the scales to actual, recognizable songs on their coronets, clarinets, and saxophones. My trombone was stuck in place, sounding more like a wounded heifer than Buddy Morrow.

Finally, after making a heroic effort, the instructor counseled my parents to give up the lessons and sell the trombone. Mother and I were in a bit of a panic, for we had persuaded my father this was a sound investment. Now we were stuck with a used trombone and the chances of getting our $90 back seemed remote. Fortunately, a local boy decided he wanted to take up the trombone and we unloaded it on his family for the purchase price. To this day, Mother and I still consider that one of the critical financial transactions of our relationship. If we had not sold the horn, Red would have raised it in every discussion of family finances.

The music gene was also missing in my par-

My brother Bill and me, with food for the table!

With my brothers, Bill and Mike.

ents and two brothers. In church we stood with the hymnals open, mute and slightly ill at ease, a cast of the musically challenged. Curiously, we all appreciate music, but I often wonder how much more we'd relish the melody if we could produce it.

Many years later I was invited to narrate Copland's "Lincoln Portrait" with the Boston Pops at a summer concert. My wife, Meredith, who is musically gifted, and two of our daughters were in the audience; as I came onstage I looked to them for reassurance but saw instead expressions of utter terror. But I was not singing, I was merely reading, and that I knew I could do. Perhaps they were afraid I might be tempted to hum along.

Since music was not an option in my young life, I had more time for other pursuits, and along the river and in the surrounding hills, I enjoyed a pioneer boyhood.

Neither my father nor my grandfather was what you would call an outdoorsman. They were the exceptions among most of the men in the places where I grew up. Hunting and fishing were an extension of breathing and eating

The summer of 1958, I was a tour guide at Gavins Point Dam. My father's boss, Bob Roper, is on the right, welcoming tourists.

in the rural areas of the Great Plains, where game was abundant and the lakes and rivers were rich with fish. I cannot remember a specific incident or person who led me into that culture, but I do know it was an important part of my young life.

Pickstown was ideally situated for anyone who wanted to get out of the house, or, in my case, out from under my father's idea of how to spend a Saturday: clean the garage, mow the lawn, build a picnic table, overhaul a car, paint a room. Work was his hobby, but I was looking for a little more adventure.

When we first arrived, Pickstown was a work in progress, a giant playground for kids. I played hide-and-seek in the framing of the cavernous movie theater while it was under construction; watched the road crews carve out grids of streets and add the pavement, curbs, and sidewalks; looked on in eager anticipation as the soda fountain was moved into the new drugstore. I watched the hospital, the hotel, the church, and the school rise out of the leveled river bluff on which the town was constructed.

In the early years I bonded with Don Stokes, the bright and adventurous son of a Corps engineer. He was seven and I was eight but we shared a thirst for excitement, and before long we were disappearing over the edge of the town and into the hills beyond, picking our way across patches of cactus and sagebrush, skirting rattlesnake dens and disappearing into steep coulees carved out of the prairie by languid creeks (which we pronounced "cricks").

We carried Red Ryder model BB guns and managed to become so accurate we could hit sitting grasshoppers and even houseflies when they settled down. We longed for bigger game—rabbits and squirrels—but Red Ryder did have its limits. Nonetheless, guns—mostly small-bore and shotguns—helped define my formative years.

When I was twelve I was bedridden with a painful case of pleurisy, probably brought on by a cold overnight camping trip with only a thin Army surplus sleeping bag for warmth. Not much could comfort me until my father presented me with the classic Marlin .22 lever-action rifle he had inherited from his mentor, Oscar Johnson. I kept it in bed with me until my recovery, which I am sure was speeded by my eagerness to step up from the BB gun.

Weekends, especially during the cold winter months, I'd head off into the hills or thick

woods with my friends Bobby Gene Davenport and Jerry Brentesen to shoot squirrels and
rabbits or to shoot at targets in improvised con-
tests. We'd discuss the latest .22 automatic
someone had spotted in the new Sears cata-
logue and wonder how we could earn enough
money to buy it. Mostly, however, we were
content with what we had, which included
single-shot .22s. These rifles forced the shooter
to take great care with his aim, for a miss
meant no second chance.

One of the rites of passage for a South Dakota
male is pheasant hunting in the expanses of
corn fields, sorghum, wetlands, and tall prairie
grass. Since my dad didn't hunt, neighbors and
friends' fathers included me in their Saturday
excursions stalking the wily and colorful bird,
which was introduced in the Dakotas in the
early twentieth century.

We were country-boy hunters without fancy
dogs or custom-made guns. Pump shotguns
and clothing from the Army surplus store was
all we needed on those golden Saturday afternoons in the days before farmers began charging for access to their fields. The musty smell
of testosterone and the sharp scent of cordite
were in the air as we crawled over barbed-wire

fences and pushed through corn stalks, mur-
muring, "Up, bird, up, bird," a call I suspect
did little to arouse the cunning pheasants. Still,
the whirring sound of a cackling cock pheasant exploding out of a hiding place remains as
familiar to me as the sound of, say, a fire siren
marking high noon in small towns.

At the end of the day, hunting was more than
sport. It was a serious matter of balancing the
cost of shotgun shells against the gain in food
on the table. Pheasant dinners were a staple of
our autumn diet, and they weren't the elegant
presentations I later came to appreciate in
high-end big-city restaurants. In some families,
pheasant was cooked like chicken: dusted with
flour or cornmeal and fried in Crisco. I preferred the Campbell's mushroom soup version.
Fill a roasting pan with pheasant breasts (the
other parts were too tough) and cover with
mushroom soup. Bake and serve.

While guns were an integral part of our
working-class environment, they generated
none of the impassioned debate heard on both
sides of the equation today. They were for
hunting and target shooting. In contrast to my
later life, as a child I knew of no one using a
gun in anger. Gun safety was a conspicuous part

of the introduction of guns to a member of a family, but that didn't head off all accidents.

One night I returned home to find my parents in my room, looking at once anxious and angry. My father was plastering over a large hole in the wall. My brother Mike, then just eight years old, had gotten my .410 shotgun out of its hiding place in the back of the closet, found the shells, loaded the gun, and fired a round into the wall. He had been waiting for a chance to fire the gun and when my father told him he was too young, he seized his own opportunity when my parents and I were out. After that close call, the guns and ammo were locked away.

One of my sixth-grade classmates, an overweight and clumsy child, accidentally shot himself in the shoulder while leaning on his shotgun to tie a shoe. We were sympathetic during visits to his hospital room, but astonished that he would do something quite so dumb.

In 1968, when there was so much violence in America, including the deaths of two men I greatly admired—Dr. Martin Luther King, Jr., and Robert F. Kennedy—I gave away my two shotguns and one .22 rifle to an NBC News cameraman. I stopped shooting for twenty-five years, until we had a ranch in Montana and a one-of-a-kind yellow Labrador retriever, Sage, the wonder dog.

Now I return annually to South Dakota for fall pheasant hunting trips with boyhood friends and relatives, driving to the fields in expensive SUVs, shooting expensive foreign-made over-and-under shotguns on land reserved for our party. Sage and Abby, our black Labrador, bred and trained in Scotland, flush and retrieve the birds. At the end of the day we retire to comfortable houses in Sioux Falls to drink single-malt scotch and eat braised pheasant breast sans mushroom soup, silently toasting the social evolution of our little South Dakota piece of the working class.

I go through the looking glass, too, when I pack my tubes of expensive fly rods, waders, assorted paraphernalia, and favorite fishing vest and head off to an exotic location for freshwater or saltwater fly-fishing. It's a long way from the inexpensive rods and reels of my youth, which came only after an introductory season on a cane pole.

No one else in my family cared for fishing any more than they did for hunting, so again I am not sure how the desire was born. But I was determined to become an angler. My parents would drive me to nearby Lake Andes, where for fifteen cents I could buy a bucket of minnows from a kindly farm woman named Gladys Wilson and fish from her dock. I'd eat my lunch and, when I had a stringer full of crappies or bluegills, I'd walk out to the highway and hitchhike eight miles home on those days when my parents were otherwise busy.

Missouri River fishing in those days before the massive dams altered the water flow was an ichthyologist's smorgasbord. On a single day of slinging weighted hooks loaded with juicy night-crawler worms into the swift currents, an enterprising fisherman could catch a sturgeon, catfish, sauger, drum (a kind of river bass), skipjack, eel, and smallmouth bass.

I became so obsessed with fishing that my mother gently suggested I was shirking my chores at home. I responded with twelve-year-old righteous indignation, "Hey, I'm putting food on the table!" That drew a laugh, but in the end I went back to my chore list.

However, I could not be confined to the house or yard for long, not when there was so much to explore just outside of town. Trained geologists were an important part of the Corps of Engineers workforce, and they organized a club for those of us interested in collecting fossils and rocks and minerals.

With a couple of pals, I scoured the glacial till that made up the river's boundaries, picking up banded agates, petrified wood, obsidian, jasper, and white quartz. With my friends Warren Fisk and Chuck Englund, I cut and polished the better specimens, even turning out a pair of handsome agate earrings for my mother.

But for the most part, I was simply interested in amassing a large collection from the rich geology surrounding me. To this day I could take a stranger to the best collection points in the bluffs along the river, including one that Warren and I dubbed Secret Hill because it gave up so many kinds of petrified wood, a chunk of which sits in my Park Avenue living room.

Warren and I had one bonanza summer when the Corps dredged out the area below the dam to create a channel for the discharge from the big hydroelectric turbines. The residue from the dredging was forced out onto a floodplain at the river's edge; as soon as the water drained away, Warren and I would be on our hands and knees, crawling across the muddy landscape, looking for new treasures. We recovered buffalo skulls, Indian artifacts, including a beautiful sweetwater agate hide scraper, what appeared to be the petrified foreleg of some ancient animal, and sacks full of agates and pieces of obsidian.

To this day I cannot walk across a graveled driveway or hillside anywhere without looking down, hoping I'll spot a rock worth keeping. And during a lifetime of travel, I have visited rivers the world over that in one way or another take me back to the banks of the Missouri. I scour the sandbars and gravel deposits for mineral keepsakes, calculate the speed of the currents, size up the backwaters and eddies, and always marvel at these ancient arteries of nature, coursing through the landscape without pause, night and day.

I have always identified with that passage in *The Adventures of Huckleberry Finn* in which Huck describes life on the river with Jim. "We catched fish and talked, and we took a swim now and then to keep off sleepiness. It was kind of solemn, drifting down the big, still river, laying on our backs looking up at the stars. . . ." Any boy on a river on a summer night is part Huck Finn.

Yet I was also driven to make money at an early age. I had a lawn-mowing business that expanded considerably the summer Red built me a power lawn mower from parts in his garage. He mounted a small gasoline engine from an old washing machine on a plywood platform and connected it to a blade he hand tooled. The platform wheels were from a child's wagon, and Dad welded some pipes together to make the handle. It was the Sherman tank of mowers and with it I did steady business from June through August.

I also set pins in the bowling alley for a dime a line, a hot and demanding task that required jumping into a pit to collect the downed pins and loading them back into the heavy metal rack before the next ball was rolled. I ran errands for neighbors and delivered sales pamphlets for local merchants. But on weekends I'd head into the woods or hills surrounding our little outpost of modern civilization.

It's not surprising, given my interests in the outdoors and in social gatherings, that at an early age I became an enthusiastic member of the scouting movement. Mother was our local den mother for the Cub Scouts, and I quickly made my way through all the stages, eager to move from those blue uniforms to the khaki brown of the Boy Scouts. The Scouts were a big part of my early teens, with their emphasis on outdoor skills, community service, and recognition of achievement in the form of merit badges. It was a natural fit with my "good boy" reputation.

The Boy Scouts and town baseball programs, community dances, and school citizenship awards were all sponsored by the local post of the American Legion, the most popular of the post–World War II veterans' organizations. The Legion was a very substantial presence, but I don't recall any overt ideological crusades on its part. Everyone in town shared a sense of patriotism, and the Pledge of Allegiance was a daily classroom ritual.

I was not a perfect child; I loved harmless mischief and I got into more than my share of playground fights, but the idea of rebelling against convention or authority was not in my makeup. In those years not too long after World War II, when America was still greatly influenced by the military discipline that millions of veterans had brought home to civilian life, I was a young foot soldier, pleased that I measured up to expectations. I was entirely comfortable in the Boy Scout uniform and uniformity.

I was appointed a senior patrol leader, the Boy Scout equivalent of a colonel running a battalion, when I was thirteen. The "promotion" had an immediate effect. I liked the leadership role and quickly stepped away from the high jinks in the ranks so my peers would take me more seriously. I became a member of the Order of the Arrow, a sort of Phi Beta Kappa for Scouts, and I liked wearing its distinctive white banner.

Scouting also gave our forays into the nearby hills and along the river real purpose. We'd work on our merit badges during overnight camping trips, lugging our gear in Army surplus packs and trying to stay warm in cheap Army blanket sleeping bags. A favorite spot was out of sight of town, beneath a lone oak tree on the bank of a prairie creek, not too far from an artesian well. This was our Everest base camp. We wore the ground smooth over several summers and autumns as we set up pup tents and built fire rings for meals of Brunswick stew, pork chops, and vegetables wrapped in foil and baked in the smoldering coals. For dessert we had marshmallows and melted Hershey chocolate bars.

In my fifties, I returned to those familiar hills and found my way to a spot across from the tree. The grass had grown back to waist height and the tree was even more stately after another forty years of growth. As I took in the scene, I thought for a moment I could see several twelve-year-old boys scurrying around, gathering firewood, drinking from canteens, and checking their .22s. But in a blink, they were gone, sent back to the memory cell from which they had emerged so briefly.

The Boy Scouts gave me a ticket out of town and what passed for a summer of adventure when I was just fifteen. I was hired as an assistant waterfront instructor at Camp Shetek, a lakeside Boy Scout facility in southwestern Minnesota. The other counselors were all in their late teens or early twenties, so it was a heady experience to spend a summer away from home in their company.

They were idyllic days, spent in T-shirts and shorts or swimming suits, starting with early-morning flag raising and ending with taps. In between I taught swimming, canoeing, and rowing before lifeguarding for the afternoon general swim session. I worked on my tan more than on my merit badges and was diverted from my Eagle Scout course by my interest in a slightly older girl in a nearby town who advanced my understanding of making out at the local drive-in movie theater.

That early exposure to lifeguarding gave me a heightened sensitivity to the possibility of trouble whenever I visited a swimming area. As a teenager I pulled a few errant youngsters out of water deeper than their swimming abilities, but it wasn't until I was in my early twenties that I had the ultimate test.

I had gone to a swimming area along the Missouri River in Yankton to have a dip and study for summer classes during my senior year in college. I chose an isolated area well beyond the roped-off safe swimming section and spread out my things on the beach. Suddenly, over the raucous clamor of the kids in the designated area, I could hear a frantic cry of "Help!" I looked out to an isolated stretch of water just in time to see a man flapping his arms as he disappeared beneath the surface. No one else seemed to notice.

I ran up the beach, yelling at some bathers to call the police, and then plunged in, swimming to where I thought he had disappeared. I dove under, but there was no sign of him in the murky river water. When I surfaced, a rotund man on shore yelled to me to try further to my right. I dove again and my leg kicked a body. I grabbed the submerged figure around his chest and started for the surface. When we broke free, his eyes rolled back and there was a huge exhalation of air. I yelled at him, "Buddy, we're gonna make it."

I was wrong. He was dead. Once ashore, I worked on him until the paramedics arrived, and they worked for another fourty-five minutes, but it was too late. I later learned he was a graduate student in math at the University of South Dakota, an Iowa resident who hoped to teach.

During the summer I worked at Camp Shetek, nothing that dramatic or draining occurred. I lived in a tent next to the swimming docks and canoe racks for two months, sharing the site with two bright college students, Dan Martensen and Mike Rogness, and my tentmate, Eldon Eisenach, a brilliant high school senior from Yankton, South Dakota. Dan, Mike, and Eldon spent the summer reading War and Peace, Crime and Punishment, and other thick tomes well beyond my sphere of interest at the time. But I loved to sit in on their lively discussions of the relative merits of the books and their spirited arguments on Protestant theology.

Dan and Mike were serious students of Luther. Eldon's father was a theology professor at a small Congregational college. The Lutherans were not much taken with the more laissez-faire attitude of the Congregationalists. Eldon, so far as I could tell, more than held his own. He later went to Harvard, earned a Ph.D. in political science at Berkeley, and has spent his life in higher education.

It was 1955. Eisenhower was getting ready to run for a second term and my beloved Dodgers were on track to win their first World Series. In the American South, the long struggle for Negro rights was gaining momentum thanks to *Brown v. Board of Education*. Perón was on his way out in Argentina, and Richard J. Daley was on his way into City Hall in Chicago.

For me, however, the real legacy of the summer grew out of a ritual we conducted in our tent most nights. Eldon had brought to camp his trombone, and each night he took out of the trombone case a picture he kept in it of a girl he was dating back home. At midsummer, though, she wrote him a "Dear John" letter, and I helped him compose a devastatingly sarcastic response.

My life was about to change profoundly, in ways I could not have imagined. My parents arrived at camp to tell me we were leaving Pickstown. We were moving to the largest town in which we'd ever lived: Yankton, a modern little city with a high school enrollment of four hundred! I was afraid I'd get lost in study hall.

"Well," I thought, "I know two people in Yankton: Eldon—and the girl in the trombone case." Her name was Meredith Auld.

CHAPTER 7

Yankton

SOMETIME IN AUGUST OF MY FIFTEENTH
year, I hitched a ride from Pickstown with a
departing family and got off in Yankton, my
new home. I felt like Benjamin Franklin arriving in Philadelphia as I walked up Maple Street
to the home of friends where my father was
staying until he could find a place for our family. I had a ducktail haircut and a new pair of
white buck shoes in my wardrobe. I was ready
for the big time.

Yankton had been the capital of the Dakota
Territory before statehood, and over the past
seventy-five years it had grown. It had good
public schools, two colleges, good medical services, a substantial hospital, a daily newspaper,
two radio stations, and a Norman Rockwell

main street of shops, banks, cafés, and bars, all arranged along the banks of the Missouri River.

As part of its historic past, Yankton could claim the ill-fated General George C. Custer. He camped there one spring and summer before heading west for the encounter at Little Big Horn. A billboard at one end of town featured a large caricature of Custer saying "Shore wish Ah'd stayed."

Mother and Dad bought their first home, a two-story, three-bedroom house on a corner lot at 1515 Mulberry. They paid $11,500. The rooms were small and the house had only one bathroom, but we had a large backyard and a two-car garage. Our house was a solid symbol of working-class success, and an important statement of stability, because there was some skepticism in Yankton about the arrival of Corps of Engineers and construction families.

The city was not accustomed to a sudden influx of new residents. Indeed, there were rumors that local employers feared that the higher wages of the construction workers and Corps of Engineers employees at the dam would put pressure on them to raise pay. On Main Street and beyond, hired help often received the minimum wage, which was raised

WE ARE PROUD
OF THE HONORED FEW
WHO LEAD
OUR SCHOOL INTO VIEW

My senior-year honors picture, 1958,
taken when I was already heading
for a crash landing.

in 1955 from 75 cents to $1 an hour. But Yankton's initial wariness quickly gave way to a recognition that the newcomers shared local values and, just as important, had steady paychecks, which improved the economic prospects of the town.

I was at once excited and a little apprehensive about the move. Yankton had been one of our "big city" shopping and recreation destinations, so it always seemed a little exciting to me. After all, it had three movie theaters, more than one gasoline station, several grocery stores, and a country club, for God's sake. Actually, the golf course was just nine holes and the clubhouse was little more than a meeting room, but it was a dividing line in the town, between the white-collar professionals and the blue-collar, hourly wage residents.

Yankton was mostly a blue-collar town, but it had more variety than Pickstown. I'd be going to school with the children of physicians, lawyers, bankers, broadcasters, professors, and merchants as well as the working class. Also, there seemed to be a lot of those children. My new high school was four times the size of my last one, and it had a reputation for athletic and academic prowess.

OUR WANTED GOAL IS FINALLY ATTAINED
AFTER TWELVE YEARS OF BEING TRAINED

MEREDITH AULD Debate 1-4; NFL 1-4; Cheerleader 2-4, Capt. 4; Chorus 1-2; All-State Chorus 1; Jr. Play; Quill & Scroll 3-4; Latin Club 3-4; Woksape 3-4; Declam 1-2; All-School Play Co-Director 4; Stud. Gov. 3-4; Arickara Attendant; Girls State 3; Girls Nation; Hobbies: Music.

TOM BROKAW Football 2-4; Track 2-4; Hmr. Pres. 2-4; Pres. Stud. Council 4; Mardi Gras Cand. 2-3; Woksape 2-4; Annual 3; Arickara Nominee 4; Boys State 3; "Y" Club 4; Quill & Scroll 4; Jr. Play; All-School Play 4; NFL 4; Canteen Council 2; Hobbies: records, dancing.

Two classmates—later two mates in life.

My friend Eldon from Boy Scout camp was a big help, wryly dissecting the social strata of the student population and faculty, separating the dumb jocks from the interesting ones, and applying the same standards to the girls. Who was smart and pretty and who was merely pretty, who was rumored to be promiscuous, a word that was new to me even if the condition was not.

It was a heady time for me. I plunged into my first experience with eleven-man football; a homeroom where I was elected president my first day in class; the teen canteen, a run-down but comfortable hangout with Ping-Pong, beat-up pool tables, and an excellent jukebox that pumped out the early classics of rock and roll as well as the standards of Sinatra, Dean Martin, and Patti Page for slow dancing.

As a new member of the student council (because of my homeroom presidency), I was selected to raise the flag in front of the school every morning. My partner was Hal Brost, a truly big man on campus. He was an All-State tackle on the football team and he was headed for the Air Force Academy. Hal persuaded me that chinos were more appropriate wardrobe than blue jeans for students with responsibility, and I happily went along.

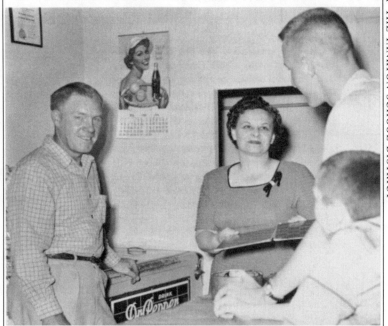

*Mother and Dad helping out
at Yankton's Teen Canteen, 1958.*

The ducktail haircut and white bucks disappeared after the first school assembly. When I walked into the auditorium, Roger Lowe, a golden boy for his football heroics and blond good looks, said aloud, "Who in the hell is *that?*" Roger became one of my best friends, a surrogate son in our family, but he never tired of sharing his first impression of me.

I quickly discovered that I had moved into a much more competitive environment. There were many more than just one or two bright kids in Yankton High, and they had grown up with much better study habits than I had developed in the more relaxed environs of Pickstown. It was my first experience with being just another fish in the pond.

Many of my friends were upperclassmen, including Eldon, a senior, and Don Trebilcock, another senior. Don and I had shared a seat on a long bus ride back from a basketball game and discovered we had similar interests, even though he was two years older, a significant gap during high school years. His family had an impressive book and music collection, and I can still remember going to their pine-paneled basement to hear a recording by the great blues singer Joe Williams for the first time. I was six-

BID GOODBYE TO YANKTON HIGH SCHOOL

Yankton High School graduation day, 1958.
That's me, holding on to the tassel.
I was headed to the University of Iowa—
and a wake-up call.

Commencement

Processional ------------------------------- High School Band
Invocation --------------------------- The Rev. L. W. Sachse
Band: "Toccata" --------------------------------- Frescobaldi
Presentation of Speaker ------------- Mr. Lester H. Baumann
Commencement Address: ------------- Mr. Herbert E. Evans
     Vice President-General Manager
     Peoples Broadcasting Company
Chorus: "Prayer" --------------------------- Mascagni-Cain
   "Almighty God of Our Fathers" --------------- James
Presentation of Class ------------------ Mr. Don R. Snowden
Presentation of Diplomas ------------------ Dr. Merritt Auld
Benediction ----------------------- The Rev. L. W. Sachse

teen, and his song "Every Day I Have the Blues" is permanently fixed in my memory.

One of the most remarkable changes in my life was the ability to watch the news on television every night. I was a sophomore when Chet Huntley and David Brinkley made their debut on NBC; they quickly became a fixture in our home. Supper was served at five, and at five-thirty we watched *The Huntley-Brinkley Report,* which was a window on a world we had never seen before except in Movietone newsreels at the local movie theater.

Life in Yankton may have been routine, but beyond our borders the world was changing in great, convulsive shudders. In Eastern Europe the most serious challenge to Moscow since the end of World War II was under way in Hungary, where students and workers demanded their rights. We cheered them on from afar; when they were crushed by a massive Soviet invasion while the United States and NATO stood by, it was a sobering lesson in the nuclear realities of the Cold War.

In the American South the first stirrings of the civil rights revolution were being felt in Montgomery with the bus boycott inspired by Rosa Parks and led by a young Negro minister,

Yankton High School

THIS CERTIFIES THAT

Thomas John Brokaw

HAS COMPLETED THE COURSE OF STUDY AS PRESCRIBED
BY THE BOARD OF EDUCATION FOR THE HIGH SCHOOL
DEPARTMENT AND IN RECOGNITION OF MERITORIOUS
ATTAINMENTS IN SCHOLARSHIP IS AWARDED THIS

DIPLOMA

GIVEN AT YANKTON, SOUTH DAKOTA,
THIS TWENTY-SEVENTH DAY OF MAY, 1958.

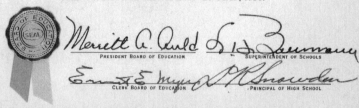

PRESIDENT BOARD OF EDUCATION   SUPERINTENDENT OF SCHOOLS

CLERK BOARD OF EDUCATION   PRINCIPAL OF HIGH SCHOOL

Dr. Martin Luther King, Jr. President Eisenhower sent federal troops to Little Rock so Negro students could attend Central High School. Even though we saw the rage, the anguish, the fear on our television screens, we seemed far removed from the consequences.

A great pall was lifted from America with the introduction of the Salk vaccine, the breakthrough drug in preventing the childhood curse of polio. *Marty, East of Eden, The Seven Year Itch,* and *Rebel Without a Cause* came to our movie theaters. Don Trebilcock and I affected an Ernest Borgnine–as–Marty style when we checked in with each other. "Whatta ya wanna do tonight?" "I dunno, Marty, whatta *you* wanna do?" Most nights we did the same thing: we dragged the main street in his 1949 Ford, listening to Elvis, Buddy Holly, Chuck Berry, Fats Domino, and Pat Boone trying to do the white man's version of "Tutti Frutti."

The arrival of rock and roll changed more than the musical rhythms of America. Until Elvis, my generation had been in lockstep with our parents: big bands and crooners singing love songs. Suddenly, rebellion was in vogue, from music to films and comedy. It was slightly disorienting for me. I loved the new music and

I was entranced by the brooding intensity of James Dean in *Rebel Without a Cause,* but I was the apotheosis of the establishment teenager with a crew cut who played by the rules—most of the time, anyway. I didn't like it when girls were drawn to the obscure guys with long hair and hot rods as much as they were to the jocks with letter jackets and hand-me-down family sedans.

While I was in high school, the novel *Peyton Place,* about the social and sexual hypocrisy of a small New England town, caused a great stir across the country, including in Yankton. We were not altogether innocent of the same sins. Teenage pregnancies and grown-up affairs were hushed up in the common determination to present Yankton as an all-American city, an honor *Look* magazine accorded it the year after we arrived.

It was not unusual or inappropriate for residents to see in Yankton what they wanted. It had long been a city of strong faith, with a sizable Roman Catholic population that peacefully co-existed with the more numerous Protestants. Yet some parents preferred that their children date only within the faith. As one of the few Protestants on the basketball team, I developed a taste for fish sticks thanks to Friday pregame meals with my Catholic teammates.

Since Yankton was once a rough-and-tumble frontier town, drinking establishments were a fixed part of the landscape. There were no fewer than six bars on the three-block-long main street, and several on the side streets.

When I returned to Yankton to film a profile on my hometown for the *Today* show's bicentennial series in 1976, I showed a clip from one of the favorite drinking places, a carryout beer joint, an act of high heresy according to some of the town's leading figures.

One of my favorite hangouts was a combination pool hall and bar called Bud's Snooker. It had eight snooker and pool tables arranged in one row in a long, narrow room that always smelled of tobacco smoke and stale beer. The bar served ten-cent glasses of beer (sometimes mixed with tomato juice), cold Polish sausages, and hardboiled eggs—a wicked prescription for nuclear flatulence.

The pool hall protocol was fixed, if not written down. As your skills developed, you worked your way up to table one, the first and largest of the snooker tables. Snooker, with smaller pockets and more complicated rules, was a much more sophisticated game than straight pool, and table one credentials were unspoken but accepted by consensus of the other shooters.

Every game generally involved some kind of a bet, if for nothing more than the cost of the game. Sometimes $20 would be on the table, a big bet in those days, and such occasions provided lasting lessons in human nature and gambling. One of my friends was a good player, but more important, he had the heart of a gambler and the bank account of a car dealer's son. He often played against a laborer who was his equal in snooker and needed the money more than my friend did. Invariably, the laborer lost because he choked under pressure, while the car dealer's son played with the confidence of a shooter who knew there were more $20 bills at home.

A few Yankton families did have money, but no one was really rich and even those with money were careful not to flaunt it.

Most people had modest or low incomes, and the distinction was so small that there was little sense of a class system. I now realize that several of my friends came from families that were, objectively speaking, poor; the kids all worked after school and held summer jobs not for a little extra spending money but to help their family get by from week to week. (One of those friends left right after high school to go work for a supermarket chain in California. He stayed with the company for more than twenty-five years, collecting stock as he went along. Finally, the chain sold in one of those big mergers of the nineties and my friend walked away with $20 million. His deserved good fortune cheers me every time I think about it.)

In our family, Mother and Dad's resourcefulness ensured that we always had what we needed. Like their friends, they could recite the price of every piece of produce and cut of meat, every gallon of gas, set of tires, pair of shoes, and warm winter jacket for sale in town. I was more of a spendthrift, but I was never guilt-free about my waywardness with money.

At Gavins Point Dam my father was appointed foreman of the outside construction crew, a job that was tailor-made for his myriad skills and pride of workmanship. He was at once a stern taskmaster and, because of his generous spirit, a lovable boss. He and his men built riverside parks and camping sites that still draw compliments now, more than forty years after they were constructed. Dad—Red—treated them like extensions of our home. On many a summer night he'd grab me for a late-night tour of the sites to make sure that everything was in its place and the campers had what they needed.

My first summer in Yankton, I landed an ideal job: running a boat dock and bait shop below the dam on the river. I used to say I was paid $35 a week and all the minnows I could eat. I sold fishing tackle, minnows, and night crawlers, rented out the boats, and swam off the dock when business was slow. The county sheriff stopped by most mornings to check on the fishing and to recite the overnight crime log, which usually amounted to a misdemeanor or two.

The owner of the enterprise, a crusty jack-of-all-trades named Bob Sherman, operated a well-worn combination gas station and sporting goods shop near the railroad tracks. Bob was a man of few words and I was my usual chatterbox self, but we got along well because I was handy with boats and honest at the cash register, a trait he later told me was rare among the part-timers he had hired over the years. He had a tough-guy reputation but he gave me the use of a 1935 Ford pickup and any of the boats when I wasn't on duty.

I was playing shortstop on the local American Legion baseball team and working a couple of nights at the local radio station, spinning records and broadcasting news from the local public high school and the local Catholic school for girls. Saturdays I had a job at a men's store where I was one of three salesclerks, with the owner and his one full-time employee.

My pals would drift through the store on Saturday to gossip about sports and girls. For some reason, all of the guys had to have a nickname. There was a Rocky, a Moose, Barnacle Bill, Cherokee, Tidy, Horny, Lefty, Skeeter, Doc, Pudgy. To some I was known as Kawbro, a reversal of my last name's syllables. To this day we still all refer to each other by those names. "Moose" is a distinguished lawyer in Chicago and "Rocky" has made his mark in university relations in Washington and San Francisco. When I see them in their professional settings and call them by their high school nick-names, their colleagues are always a little puzzled.

By my junior year in high school I felt as if we had been living in Yankton forever. I was elected president of the class, and the vice president was that beautiful and studious girl Meredith Auld. We also had the leads in the class play, and when I suited up for football and basketball games she was a cheerleader on the sidelines. She was dating one of my best friends, so we saw each other regularly but we were no more than friends. She was cheerfully wary of my reputation as a teenage lothario. I liked and admired her, but as a prospective girlfriend she had too much self-control for my tastes.

She did have a humorous take on me, however. At a basketball-team pep rally during the Christmas holiday my senior year, Meredith, presiding as the captain of the cheerleaders, was handing out presents to the varsity team members. When it was my turn, Meredith revealed a sailor cap, because, she said, laughing, "Tom has a girl in every port."

In the spring of my junior year I was one of the Yankton delegates to Boys State, a week-long program sponsored by the American Legion to encourage public service. The best and brightest of the state's high school juniors assembled on a college campus for a week of debates and seminars on the public policy issues of the day. The delegates were divided and assigned to two political parties for a series of elections beginning at the local level and moving up swiftly to statewide offices.

I was the nominee in my party for governor, the big prize. My running mate was Robert Legvold, a debate champion from the big city in South Dakota, Sioux Falls. We parlayed his cool command of the issues and my knowledge of small-town South Dakota into a landslide victory. (Thirty years later, Legvold often appeared with me on *NBC Nightly News* as the Soviet Union was collapsing. He had become one of America's leading authorities on Russia and national security issues.)

When I delivered my inaugural address on statewide radio before my fellow delegates, I could see my parents at the back of the hall. They had gotten up at three A.M. for the long drive to the campus in the northern part of the state to be there for me, just as they had been there when I gave that first Christmas reading on the Army base during the war.

I had lunch with the real governor, Joe Foss, a Congressional Medal of Honor recipient in

World War II, a man's man of the highest order. He was still flying airplanes, and he was regularly featured on television hunting and fishing shows. Joe was charismatic and our state's biggest celebrity and yet he was always one of us, a plain-talking, occasionally profane ex-farmer who performed his duty magnificently in war and then returned home to a life of public service. We became instant friends at the luncheon, a relationship that continues to this day.

I was invited to appear before the delegates at Girls State the following week. One of the delegates was Meredith, who, not surprisingly, was a star of that gathering. She was selected as one of two delegates to Girls Nation, where she met President Eisenhower in the Rose Garden at the White House. When she returned, I was eager to hear her impressions, since she was the only person I had ever known who had actually met a President of the United States. She laughed and said, "He was like a grandfather—with very rosy cheeks."

My summer plans for 1957 seemed romantic at the time I made them. I was interested in a girl who was a nursing student in Rochester, Minnesota, home of the Mayo Clinic; fortuitously, my favorite aunt and uncle hired me for their small rock quarry business in northern Iowa, not too far away from Rochester. They were my mother's sister, Marcia, and her husband, Stan, a University of Texas graduate.

Marcia and Stan had a taste for the good life or, as I believe my father might have put it, "They spend it as fast as it comes in." They had one of the first models of the Ford Thunderbird and they were regulars on the dog show circuit with their prize Doberman pinschers. They liked expensive restaurants and shopping sprees in Minneapolis. They were my kind of relatives.

Marcia and Stan were determined that I have a good time living with them that summer, so they arranged a road trip to Minneapolis to hear a Harry Belafonte concert and schooled me in the ways of fine dining at Rochester's best restaurant. Sundays I'd accompany them to local church socials, where Stan would solicit customers for his business. Weeknights we'd walk down to the local café for pie and coffee and the latest gossip. They treated me more like a slightly younger brother than a nephew and I relished the notion of being a grown-up in training.

Working for the company was another matter. I was at the bottom of a rock quarry for long hours during the midsummer Iowa heat, loading crushed rock onto dump trucks for road construction, or breaking up big boulders with an air hammer. It was hard, noisy, dusty work, and next to the muscular farm boys who had done this kind of labor all of their lives, I wasn't very proficient, nor was I very enthusiastic about the drudgery.

By noon I'd be worn out and they would be diving cheerfully into lunchboxes stuffed with what looked like ten pounds of thick sandwiches and packages of Twinkies. Several had evening chores to tend to back at the farm when their long workday ended at the quarry, and yet I remember very little complaining. In their company I learned again what real work is and how it often doesn't receive the rewards it deserves.

On Saturdays I'd collect my earnings—$60 for sixty hours of work—and steer my 1946 vintage Pontiac to Rochester and a date with the nursing student, who was at best mildly interested in someone two years her junior. On the long drive back home I'd wonder how I could find some relief from the workday routine that appealed to none of my interests.

Sometime in July a call came with an offer beyond my imaginings. Back in South Dakota, Governor Foss, a major celebrity because of his World War II record, had been invited to appear on a national television quiz show, and he would need a partner. He and his friends in the American Legion, the sponsors of Boys State, decided I would be ideal. Two South Dakota governors on one screen. It meant a trip to New York for at least a couple of days.

It might as well have been a trip to the moon. The prospect of going to New York alone at the age of seventeen to appear on a national television broadcast was almost too much to take in. It was front-page news in the Yankton paper, and one of my friends immediately wrote to ask me to send a signal when I appeared by touching my left earlobe with my right hand.

Marcia and Stan took me to Rochester's best men's store to pick out a suit. The owner recommended a snazzy seersucker, saying it was all the summertime rage in New York. I opted for something more conservative, figuring it could get me through my senior year in high school and graduation.

Stan, who had been to New York, loaned me a valise and counseled me on the taxicab protocols for the trip into the city from LaGuardia Airport. I nervously followed his instructions when I arrived, directing the driver to go over the Fifty-ninth Street bridge to my hotel just off Times Square.

To this day I can remember the cabbie's friendly monologue: "Last night was so hot, ya know, I took a six-pack up to da roof and tried to sleep there but da roof is all little rocks, ya know, and it wasn't easy." He was a Brooklynite; when he learned I was from the Midwest, and that this was my first trip to New York, *and* that I was a Brooklyn Dodgers fan, he quickly became a mentor, telling me to ride subways because they're cheaper and to take a bus for my return trip to the airport for the same reason. He also had hot dog and pizza tips for Midtown and warned me about guys trying to pick up boys in Times Square.

The next thirty-six hours were dizzying. I found my way to a small office somewhere in the West Fifties for a preshow interview. The broadcast, live on CBS on Saturday nights, was

Two for the Money, starring another Midwest-erner, Herb Shriner of Ohio. He was on summer leave, so the host would be Sam Levenson, a former schoolteacher who had become famous for his witty monologues on everyday life.

The writers rehearsed me on a couple of questions Levenson was likely to ask, such as "As a teenage governor, do you have any real powers?" "What do you think of Joe Foss?" "What do you want to see in New York?" They seemed to be impressed with my ease, wished me well, and gave me the address of the studio and the time of the broadcast the following night.

I arrived in my new, sensible suit and Joe and I were assigned a dressing room to await the beginning of the live broadcast. The format was familiar: two contestants working as a team, alternating answers to a common category of questions. I was fairly certain our quiz would be heavy on politics, a subject I followed closely. Nonetheless, I made sure I knew all the states' governors and the members of Ike's cabinet.

About fifteen minutes before airtime, a nervous production assistant slipped into our dressing room. He was wearing serious tortoiseshell glasses and he had a stopwatch around his neck. He apologized for a red stain on his white shirt, explaining he'd spilled tomato sauce while eating spaghetti during the dinner break. He then began a staccato monologue that I didn't quite understand at first. "We—the show—a budget—we want you to make some money—but it's better—you know—if we have routine—so I want to try out some categories—" With that he proceeded to tell us the likely areas we'd be questioned about and suggested a few laugh lines to eat up the clock. He thought we'd make more than $1,200 between us. And then he was gone.

Joe and I were speechless. I'm not sure what he was thinking, but my first reaction was "Well, if this is the way they do it in New York, who am I to say?" It didn't seem right, but at least now I knew I wouldn't make a fool of myself.

Suddenly we were on the air and the opening patter went smoothly as I described how much it meant to a small state like South Dakota to have such a famous governor. Levenson got a laugh when he asked Joe whether, in the informal state capital, anyone ever just walked into his office and said, "Pardon me." When Joe said, "Sure," Levenson nailed the punch line: "And did you?"

When it came time for Levenson to name the categories of questions, Joe and I were not surprised to learn two of them were "Governors" and "Presidential Slogans." Joe began with Governor Goodwin Knight of California, and I responded in my best schoolboy oratorical style, "The Honorable Joe Foss of South Dakota." That got a big laugh and took some time off the clock. We had some more fun with the presidential campaign slogans and I even pulled my earlobe for my friend back home as I pondered a response. When the winnings were tallied, we had stayed within the budget, each earning a bit more than $600. The irony is that in both categories we pulled our punches; we could easily have doubled the number of correct answers.

(A few years later, when the big quiz scandals began to break, I was writing some freelance articles to earn college money. Mother called me and said, "Don't you dare write about your experience in New York. That wouldn't be fair to Joe.")

Joe had a late flight to Washington that night,

so when we left the studio he asked about my plans. I told him I was scheduled to fly back the next day but there was so much I hadn't seen in New York. He immediately said, "Oh, you should stay a few days. Call your parents and tell them I said so—and I'll see them next week in South Dakota."

That's all I needed. I raced back to the hotel and called home for a review of our performance and to make the case for staying a few extra days. When I told them the governor thought it was a good idea, there was a long pause on the other end of the phone and then my father said, "Well, I guess you should. You'll probably never get another chance to see New York."

At the time I thought he was right, and so for the next four days I slept little and saw a lot. I took a Gray Line tour of all the usual tourist spots, including Greenwich Village and Chinatown, the Statue of Liberty and the United Nations, so I could decide which I wanted to return to on my own. Not surprisingly, the Village was my first choice with its funky jazz clubs and bohemian street scene. I walked the streets until after midnight, taking in the cool riffs of laughter spilling out of sidewalk cafés

and the rich ethnic mix of the pedestrian traffic. With my very short haircut, deep midwestern tan, and schoolboy looks, I felt like a fifties
version of E.T.

I went to Saks to buy inexpensive presents
for Mother and Dad so they could at least show
off the exclusive store label, and for myself I
bought an early Japanese transistor radio at one
of those Fifth Avenue electronics stores. I went
into St. Patrick's Cathedral for my Catholic
friends and peeked into Carnegie Hall so I
could have at least a brush with New York culture. I remember thinking I could walk all day
and my feet would never leave pavement, an
experience that was absolutely contrary to my
prairie upbringing.

My big adventure, however, was a pilgrimage
to Ebbets Field the last summer my beloved
Dodgers were in Brooklyn. Jackie Robinson
had retired the year before, but many of my
other heroes were still playing, including Gil
Hodges and Duke Snider. I bought the ticket
at an agency in midtown Manhattan and the
friendly clerk wrote down the subway lines I
could take to the ballpark.

As the train approached Ebbets Field it began
to fill up with noisy Dodgers fans. I was

thrilled just to be in their company, and when I emerged from the subway to see that iconic old ballpark, I felt as if I were in a shrine, especially since the Dodgers were playing their longtime crosstown rivals, the Giants.

My seat was in the loge on the first-base side. A kindly Italian American man about my grandfather's age, in a straw hat and smoking what appeared to be a homemade crooked black cigar, spotted me as an outsider and asked how I had gotten there. I explained my South Dakota roots and my Dodgers love affair and he took me in as if I had just gotten off the boat at Ellis Island.

He pointed out Duke Snider's wife in the stands on the third-base side of the field and gave me an expert analysis of what to expect from the Dodgers manager, Walter Alston, as the innings moved along. We grudgingly admitted that Willie Mays was a heckuva player, and when a kid ran out to center field between innings to shake Willie's hand, my new friend and I joined the chorus of boos when the ushers led the young fan away.

Somehow I found my way back into midtown Manhattan on the subway after the game and got my new favorite late-night meal, an exotic dish for my South Dakota palate: a slice of pizza at a stand in Times Square. I took in the bright lights and great crowds and tried to remember it all, because, as Dad said, this might be my only chance to see New York.

CHAPTER 8

On the Air

W HEN MY FAMILY MOVED TO YANKTON, I intuitively felt we had taken a great leap upward. Not only were we able to get a television signal in Yankton, but I was living in the same community as the stars of radio station WNAX. Wynn Speece, "The Neighbor Lady," a dispenser of recipes, garden tips, and local service club news, was a fixture on South Dakota radio for half a century. One of my classmates was the son of George B. German, a former country singer who had a five-state farm following as the radio voice of "The RFD with George B." What's more, we lived just around the corner from a tidy bungalow that was once owned by Lawrence Welk, when he had the house band at WNAX in the late thirties.

WNAX was well beyond my schoolboy aspirations, but Yankton also had another, much smaller station, KYNT, which served the immediate area. It was just getting under way in 1955 with an eclectic mix of popular music, local news, high school sports, and just about anything else that might attract a sponsor.

Not long after our family arrived in Yankton, one of the KYNT disc jockeys, Harry Ebbesen, asked for teenage volunteers for a weekly show to introduce the new wave of music taking over America: rock and roll. I quickly volunteered and won the job with my sometime girlfriend, Mary Lee Keating, a bright and saucy redhead who attended the local Catholic girls' high school. (Under the "small world" heading, Mary Lee now practices at her own veterinary clinic a dozen blocks from my New York apartment.)

The relationship with Mary Lee didn't survive the year, but KYNT 1450 was a transforming experience. Vaguely, I began to think maybe this was what I was meant to do, a distant thought reinforced by my mother's daily devotion to the *Today* show with Dave Garroway and the fledgling *Huntley-Brinkley Report*. It did seem to be a kind of fantasy, so I backed it up with more conventional plans.

I thought about becoming a lawyer, maybe

Broadcasting—my ticket out of South Dakota.
At the controls of the public radio station at
the University of South Dakota.

even going into politics, or catching on with a big firm in a city such as Minneapolis, a family favorite. I wanted a life of action but I'd also been raised to look for security, that *good job* I'd heard mentioned so frequently and reverentially.

Nonetheless, I also seemed to understand almost intuitively that if journalism is what I wanted in life, I should pursue it. My parents did not overtly encourage me, but neither did they try to suppress my dreams. They nurtured them by constantly reinforcing, by example, the values of hard work and common sense. Where we lived, common sense was the coin of the realm, however elusive its exact definition. (It was a little like pornography: you knew it when you saw it.)

The radio station was on the third floor of an insurance building on Main Street. Before long I was detouring there after basketball practice and before supper to hang out with Harry; John Briggs, the station engineer, who taught me the rudiments of operating the controls; and Bill Johnson, the station manager, who doubled as the voice of high school sports broadcasts.

They were all uncommonly generous with

On a basketball road trip.
Team rules: coat and tie
when traveling.

their advice and patience as they showed me how to cue up records, maintain the logs, keep the on-air patter efficient. Instead of "It's twenty minutes to nine," I quickly learned to say, "It's eight-forty—time for this word from Randall's Super Market."

The first night Harry let me read a five-minute newscast, he stood in the other room making faces at me, trying to toughen my on-air control. I was determined not to break up, and I succeeded. However, my first line is forever etched in my memory:

"Good evening, everyone. South Dakota governor Joe Foss today addressed a convention of the Veterans of Foreign Whores." Did I say that? Yes, and in the other room my mentor was convulsed. At least I didn't break up.

By the fall of 1956, when I was sixteen, I had been working around the station long enough, usually as a volunteer, that I actually had begun to make a contribution, so Bill Johnson put me on the payroll at a dollar an hour. I filled in when disc jockeys couldn't make their night shift or on weekends, thrilled at getting paid to spin the 45 rpm records of Elvis, Bill Haley and the Comets, Fats Domino, Little Richard, Brenda Lee, Guy Mitchell, Patti Page, Peggy

Lee, Bobby Darin, and the other pop stars of the time. We didn't have a computer-generated playlist. I played what I liked and what was available in our stack of freebie records.

Even on a good night, my audience probably consisted of maybe a hundred listeners, people stuck in a passing truck, or at a gas station or in a barn somewhere on the nearby prairie, moving across the radio dial, hoping to break the monotony.

In November 1956, I had what turned out to be a life-altering experience at the station. I was asked to assist with the coverage of the 1956 presidential, congressional, and local elections. It was an opportunity for KYNT to secure its place as the voice of the community, with returns from the town and rural precincts broadcast through the night. I was assigned a rural precinct where the entire voting populace, about two dozen farm people, showed up at a one-room school lit by kerosene lamps to vote and then witness the count.

The precinct chairman invited everyone to bring a covered-dish dinner, a casserole or baked beans, and to make voting a social occasion. I pleaded with him to first count the votes and give me the tally so I could call it in.

He refused to short-circuit his routine, though; I always believed it was because he was a Democrat and he knew his precinct was going heavily for Eisenhower.

Maybe that evening was a harbinger of the debacle forty-four years later, when the decision in the presidential election of 2000 was still ambiguous the morning after Election Day as a result of vote-count chaos in Florida and a meltdown of the network vote projection system. In South Dakota on that chilly autumnal evening, at least I had a plate of hearty baked beans to temper my anxiety.

Finally, after the apple pie was finished, the vote was counted with all the voters watching. It was a heavy Republican victory. I radioed it in from my mobile unit car and raced off to the next precinct. En route I passed the home office of the local newspaper, where a reporter was marking the returns on a large exterior blackboard. "Ha," I thought, "you don't have to leave your house to hear the news on KYNT." The sight made a lasting impression on me. The world of news was moving rapidly along the electronic plane, and I was a small part of the change.

Back at the station, Bill Johnson was sitting

in his shirtsleeves before a live microphone, broadcasting the results as they were called in or ripped from the United Press International wire machine. Someone had brought in chicken dinners from Kip's Blue Moon Drive-In and there was an urn of hot coffee near the console. John Briggs was keeping us on the air and Harry Ebbesen was alternating with Bill at the mike while the sales manager made sure the commercials were read. I loved it all. I never fail to remember that night when I sit at my NBC News anchor desk during other elections, backed by thousands of colleagues, banks of screens and computers, broadcasting to a national audience.

For the next three years I worked school nights and summers at KYNT, a job that passed for glamorous in our small-town setting. It also required no heavy lifting and I could spend the sweltering summer days in air-conditioned comfort while my pals were stacking hay on nearby farms or working on road construction crews in oppressive heat. I suppose it was about then that I thought there might be something to this broadcasting business for my long-term future. And my struggles in Algebra II had quelled any thoughts of becoming a civil engineer like the role models in the construction towns where I grew up.

My early days at KYNT were also an introduction to the real business of broadcasting, which is selling airtime. Our inventive sales staff overlooked no opportunity, including fire and death. When the community fire siren went off, the automated call notifying the volunteer firemen also rang at KYNT. I would listen for the address of the call and then interrupt Elvis or Chuck Berry to broadcast something along these lines: "The fire is located at 313 Douglas. Please do not follow the fire trucks. The fire is located at 313 Douglas. Please do not follow the fire trucks." Then, after a short pause, I intoned, "Are you properly insured? For a complete line of home and business fire-insurance needs, see the Fred Leach Agency in downtown Yankton."

We sold death in comically ghoulish fashion. When the urgent bell on the UPI wire ticker rang, signaling an auto death in South Dakota, I would interrupt music programming to play prerecorded bells tolling solemnly. I faded out the bells and faded in my best seventeen-year-old funereal tones, saying, "For whom the bell tolls . . ." I gave the name of the victim and a few details of the accident before repeating, "For whom the bell tolls . . ." Fade out Tom and bring up the tolling bells again, but only for a moment. After a discreet pause, I changed to my sales pitch: "Are you properly insured? For a complete line of auto and life-insurance needs, see the Morgan T. Smith Independent Insurance Agency in downtown Yankton."

Curiously, no one objected to any of this.

Local radio was, in many ways, the central nervous system of the Midwest. Every community of any reasonable size—eight thousand people or so—had a radio station broadcasting music, news, weather, sports, and religious news. The station was a familiar and comforting voice, a kind of electronic town hall held daily, where local residents could hear about what was important in their lives.

One saloonkeeper on Main Street would often call me on summer nights to check on the Major League baseball scores. As a reward, he would let me in the back door of his establishment when my shift ended at midnight so we could share a frosted glass of beer as he closed up. (I hasten to add that this was only after I turned eighteen, the legal age for drinking 3.2 beer in South Dakota at the time.)

Baseball scores I understood. News from the local livestock markets remained a mystery even as I broadcast it. We had a remote microphone at the auction yard so the auctioneer could update our rural audience on the prices hogs and cattle were bringing. My teenage curiosity wasn't much aroused by the fate of canners and cutters, the cows sold for use in canned soups and other lesser beef products. As a town kid with big-city aspirations, I had little appreciation of the differences between farrows and lean hogs, or whether the market was steady to down. I could not have told you ten minutes after reading the number what a bushel of corn was going for on any given day. I was too eager to get back to the stack of 45s or on to the hourly newscasts that I ripped and read from the UPI ticker.

I now regret my indifference to what was going on at the stockyards and in the farms just outside the city limits. Agriculture was the foundation of the area's economy, and a good deal more complicated and challenging than playing "Young Blood" by the Coasters. My high school classmates from the farms were far more entrepreneurial than I realized as they raised a calf to a fat heifer for sale or helped their parents plant and harvest corn, soybeans, alfalfa, or sorghum.

Forty years later, at a high school reunion, I startled a classmate who had stayed on the farm by asking what it was like when he was a young man, getting up early to do chores and working weekends in the fields while the rest us dragged Main in our cars or hung out at the local drive-in. He had no idea I'd be interested in talking to anyone but the doctors, businessmen, teachers, and former cheerleaders.

Working on a farm, however, was not an option for me. You couldn't talk a corn crop to a good yield or argue a mother cow into delivering a healthy calf. I was a talker through and through, and I was happy to work longer hours to pay for button-down shirts and khaki trousers.

My Saturday job was an extension of my radio experience. I was a salesman at Hanny's Men's Wear, a no-frills clothing store on Main Street. The owner was Dwayne Hannenberger, a member of a Minnesota family that owned an upscale shop for men in Rochester. Hanny, as everyone called my boss, was new to Yankton and determined to make it on his own with his wife, Reefa, who did the books.

Hanny hired me when I was sixteen as a conduit to the high school crowd. He shrewdly realized that the high school coaches required team members to dress in jacket and tie for bus trips to away games. Since many of the high school athletes' families were working class or just plain poor, the boys didn't have a suit or tie, and very often neither did their fathers.

So in the locker room I reminded everyone that if they came to see me on Saturday at Hanny's, I could outfit them for the affordable price of $40. Hanny had a stock of boxy flannel suits in gray or black that ran $35. A shirt and tie came to an extra $5. The terms were generous: $5 down and $5 a month for seven months, no carrying charge. More than one athlete came in with his father so both could buy suits on those terms. My job was to stand off to the side and assure father and son this was the best deal in town, which it was. I think they trusted me in part because my father was one of them; he wore a hard hat and carried a lunch box every day. He had in his closet one suit and maybe three ties.

I learned a lot from Hanny about selling, although his only instructions to me were these: "Be positive" and "If someone comes in looking for a more expensive suit, come find me wherever I am." Hanny knew that buying a suit often was a once-in-a-lifetime experience in that rural culture, and he couldn't afford to miss the opportunity.

The improvisational skills I was honing on my radio shifts came in handy on Saturdays; shopping was a diversion as well as a mission for farmers and others who came to Yankton as a break from their workaday lives. They'd wander into Hanny's, "just looking," as they were likely to say, and finger the Van Heusen shirts or Sansabelt slacks.

In the beginning of the rock-and-roll era, some of the younger men from the nearby Czech American communities were "just looking" for something a little flashier. When I detected that, I took them to a back room where we kept a stash of very inexpensive shirts that had metallic threads running through them. I treated these shirts as something "very special that we don't show everyone." They were a big hit at $2.95.

As I continued to avoid manual labor by making schoolboy wages with my gift of gab, I was drawn morning and night to the black-

and-white Zenith television set in our small living room. In the morning as I crashed around, trying to get to school on time, I'd usually pause with my mother to watch a little of the *Today* show with Dave Garroway. His easy sophistication and user-friendly intelligence gave us both a lift to start the day.

Later, when I became host of *Today,* I called my mother and we recalled our shared experiences watching Garroway, Jack Lescoulie, Frank Blair, Betty Furness, and the others. They seemed like family and they took us to such interesting places. Mother remembered Garroway taking his young son on a tour of Washington, D.C., monuments; the tour left a lasting impression, because she had never seen, say, the Lincoln Memorial except in *Life* magazine or in textbooks.

Evenings, our family's appointment with Chet Huntley and David Brinkley was for me a magical experience. That fifteen-minute broadcast magnified my view over the spare prairie horizons that framed my physical existence. I was mesmerized by the nascent civil rights movement in the South. I accepted the Cold War and the possibility of nuclear war with the Soviet Union as a condition of life as

I watched Moscow brutally put down the Hungarian revolt and heard Khrushchev's promise to "bury" the West.

Television was a godsend to those of us in remote areas. It took us to places and events in the world we could no longer ignore simply because of geographical or emotional distance.

Still, I had no foreboding that the world of my innocence was coming to an end. I continued the idyllic life of a fifties teenager, working at the radio station, playing ball, chasing girls, and planning to attend college, although I wasn't sure what that meant since no one in my immediate family had gone beyond high school.

As for politics, South Dakota was a solidly Republican state with two GOP senators and a Republican governor who reflected the conservative nature of the rural population and Main Street businessmen. My parents admired Dwight Eisenhower but they voted for Adlai Stevenson a second time in 1956, their political roots in the Democratic party embedded during their struggles during the Great Depression and the long beneficial reign of Franklin Delano Roosevelt. They had good-natured arguments with their Republican friends, but it was not a blood sport, as it is in so many political dialogues today. Whatever their party registration, Mother and Dad and their friends shared more values and points of view than differences.

Sundays we watched Garroway on *Wide Wide World,* or a rising CBS star, Walter Cronkite, on *You Are There,* a re-creation of historic events, including, as I recall, the assassination of Julius Caesar. Walter, in the style that was to become so familiar and so comforting, sat off to the side, describing the events as we watched them. Now critics would laugh the show off the air, but I thought it was pretty entertaining and instructive at the same time. These experiences were leading me to a career I had not dared to consider in a serious way. Instead, I kept up my interest in current events and politics and kept on talking.

For all that I may have achieved as a journalist, to this day I am remembered in Yankton for a singular moment in my early broadcasting career. It had nothing to do with covering Dr. King for NBC, or the beginning of Ronald Reagan's rise in California. Nothing to do with covering the White House during Watergate, or with my interview with Mikhail Gor-

bachev, the first ever granted by a general sec-
retary of the Russian Communist party. I was
the only American reporter broadcasting live
from the Berlin Wall the night it came down—
but that was nothing much to those longtime
Yankton residents who remembered a summer
night in 1959.

Meredith Auld—remember?—was competing in the Miss South Dakota contest at the
other end of the state. KYNT was prepared to
stay on past midnight to report the results. I
was on duty and happily so, since I was now
dating Meredith some of the time and hoping
to improve my standing with her. As I played
records, I regularly reminded our audience
we'd have the results as soon as they were
called in.

Shortly after midnight, when I am confident
most of our listeners had stayed with us, the
phone rang. The caller was a local banker who
had accompanied Meredith to the pageant.

"She won," he said. "Would you like to
speak with the new Miss South Dakota?"

"Of course," I said, simultaneously telling
the audience that our Miss Yankton was now
Miss South Dakota, a majestic achievement in
the late fifties. Just then, Meredith came on the

air and said in what I took to be affectionate tones, "Hello, Tom."

I responded, "Hello, honey," and then, mortified by my personal lapse, I asked one quick question and signed off with "Well, there you have it—Meredith Auld, the new Miss South Dakota. Good night."

As you might expect, the next day I was the butt of a lot of jokes that went roughly, "So I stayed up past midnight so you could coo in Meredith's ear, Brokaw?" As it turns out, my relationship at the time with the new Miss South Dakota wasn't much helped by the term of endearment, but I overcame that later.

CHAPTER 9

Mother Lode

As a young white male in the fifties, I was a member of the ruling class, however inadequate my qualifications or uncertain my prospects. It was a white man's and white boy's world. Males dominated almost every aspect of American life except childbearing and mothering.

Teaching was the profession most open to women, but even there men were favored. Few women rose to be school principals or superintendents. In Yankton, where I attended high school, a male teacher was considered a "head of household" and therefore earned more than a female teacher did. Also, the school board had a policy of only one teaching job per family; if a married couple were both teachers, he got the job and she had to find another line of work.

Yankton was a thriving commercial and medical center and the seat of county government, so it had a bustling main street, a substantial hospital, an active courthouse, two banks, two high schools, and a daily newspaper. It also had just one woman doctor, no women lawyers, no women as county commissioners or city council members, just one woman on the school board, and no women who owned and operated their own businesses other than beauty shops. Women were critical to the functioning of all aspects of the community but they were almost always cast in support roles. Whatever power they had was cumulative, not assigned.

That lone woman physician, a popular and gifted pediatrician, was paid at half the rate of her male partners in a medical clinic, one of whom was her own brother, Merritt Auld, later my father-in-law. Marian Auld said later it was a difficult time for a professional woman because she had no one to turn to for guidance or comfort. (I hasten to add, in fairness to Merritt, that he later became a leading champion of equal pay for women teachers and fought hard to get women's sports introduced

*My grandmother Ethel Conley in
1929, a city girl who adjusted
to country life.*

into South Dakota high schools. When Meredith, his daughter, opened her own small chain of toy stores in New York, no one was more supportive than Merritt.)

In high school, the community pattern was repeated. Boys were favored. They had the only athletic teams, which were the pride of the town and received the most resources. Girls were cheerleaders.

Girls ran the newspaper and edited the yearbook. They were stars on the debate team and in music. They held class office, and they were far better behaved. But they were not rewarded for their excellence as their male classmates were.

In my three years at Yankton High, two of my classmates were recruited and enrolled at Harvard because of their academic promise. Two of my teammates went to Big Ten schools on athletic scholarships. Two more of my friends went to service academies, one to West Point and the other to the Air Force Academy. That's an enviable record for a high school with an enrollment of just four hundred.

They were all young men. I've often pondered how much more impressive the record could have been if similar opportunities had been available to our gifted female classmates. Instead, most them were expected to go to college to get a teaching degree and what my wife called "an MRS degree."

In our household, we had a slightly different take on the place of women in society. Since my father had effectively been raised in a sister-hood, relying on his sisters for maternal love and guidance as a youngster, he had an enlight-ened attitude about gender roles in life. It was helped by his marriage to my mother, a re-sourceful woman who was sort of the chief operating officer of the family.

Mother and Dad had been raised on the same work ethic, so there were no rigid divisions of labor, either. Housework, for example, was gender-free. If Dad arrived home before Mother, who always had a paying job of some kind, he began preparing supper. After all those early years living in the family-run hotel, he was a skilled housekeeper, so the three Brokaw boys grew up holding a vacuum cleaner or a dust rag and suffering from dishpan hands.

Mother set up an informal training course in household skills. Besides learning how to wash and iron our own shirts and trousers and sew on a button, we learned to dust the corners of the wooden stairs, set a table, wash and dry dishes, prepare simple meals, and shop for bargains.

Housekeeping was ingrained in me. Years later, while living in California, I had guests over after a tennis match. Sitting around a large glass coffee table and having snacks, we fell into a spirited discussion. Suddenly I arose from the table, kept on talking, walked to the kitchen, returned with a Windex bottle, and began to erase a spot on the glass, never losing my place in the discussion. My friends were astonished that I saw nothing unusual in my behavior.

Mother's influence went well beyond household chores, of course. In a way I came to appreciate only later, she was the reactor in our nuclear family, making sure all of the potential volatility was organized in a useful fashion. Being the only woman in a household with a strong husband and three rambunctious sons was never easy, but it was a measure of her effectiveness that we functioned smoothly as a family even during difficult times.

The greatest crisis came when my father, after many years of heavy lifting and manual labor, had to undergo a back operation that immobilized him for three months. We were living in Pickstown then, and his condition raised serious questions about whether he could continue as an employee of the Corps of Engineers.

Mother, who was working at the Pickstown post office, managed to care for him, tend to the needs of my brothers and me, and still report for her own job every day. She enlisted my help when it was time to turn Dad in the bed to which he was confined during those long, hot summer days and nights. Later I understood how anxious both of them were about their future, but Mother, especially, never let on.

Dad made a full recovery and his superiors arranged for him to move to lighter duties while he regained his strength. One of them made it clear they not only liked his work ethic and skills, but they admired his family. I am confident that was a tribute to Mother and her pivotal role in shaping our lives, including my father's.

He could have an explosive temper, especially when Bill, Mike, or I didn't measure up to his expectations about household chores or thrift. After one volcanic eruption, I complained to Mother that it seemed to be an excessive reaction to whatever shortcoming I had demonstrated. She quietly said to me, "You must remember, dear, your father grew up without a family. It's sometimes hard for him to adjust his thinking to the rest of us."

It was an instructive observation for me, a fifteen-year-old. I loved my father deeply and greatly admired him, but I didn't always share his view of what kind of work counted. Mother's commentary didn't end my confrontations with Dad but it kept me from being estranged from him during our clashes.

Also, because of Mother I think Dad came to understand the dynamics of family life; he was constantly evolving as a father and a husband. Red was the classic tough guy with a soft heart. He was more vulnerable than I realized, unable to completely shed that difficult childhood of too much hard labor and not enough open affection. Mother steered him through that with a deft touch.

Bill and Mike had their own distinctive, winning personalities and interests which didn't always match mine. As they trailed me through school or community activities, someone would say—more than they liked, I am sure—"Well, Tom did it *this* way." Mother was always quick to defend them and encourage them to do it *their* way. As the firstborn, and as someone with big ambitions, I was always determined to be at the head of whatever parade happened to be passing through my life at any given time. That did not go unnoticed, but when people told Mother, "You must be so proud of Tommy," she would say, "Yes, but you know I have two other sons, and they all make me proud."

She was one woman living with four guys in a house with one bathroom. It helped, of course, that she had a wonderful sense of self. She carved out her place in our very male bastion, working hard on table manners and social sensibilities, making astute observations about cultural developments, laughing at our locker-room humor but correcting us when it went too far. Occasionally she'd complain, with a laugh, that she wished she could have at least one daughter. But we were at least entertaining for her, even when we were not on our best behavior. She still likes to tell the story of a neighbor who came over while we were preparing to move.

He told Mother how much he'd miss us. "Well, that's so touching, Dan," she replied.

He said, "Oh, don't get the wrong idea. What I'll miss are those moments after supper when I come out on the back porch and watch Red throw the three boys out into the backyard so they can continue their fight there."

Mother sharpened my interest in national politics and popular literature. I was just eleven years old when one of the family favorites, President Harry Truman, fired General Douglas MacArthur as commander of Allied forces in Korea. It was a controversial decision, but Mother explained to me as if I were a grown-up that President Truman had done the right thing because MacArthur had, in effect, challenged his authority as commander in chief. Besides, I think she didn't approve of MacArthur's flamboyant style.

She bought Herman Wouk's *The Caine Mutiny* when it was first published, and she steered me to Hemingway's *The Old Man and the Sea*. John Steinbeck was another favorite author, and when we drove through Minnesota she would point out Sauk Centre, Sinclair Lewis's hometown, which finally, begrudgingly, acknowledged his local roots once the anger cooled over his depiction of the community as Gopher Prairie in his book *Main Street*.

For me, Mother was an early role model as a journalist even though she never worked in the field. It had been her dream, when she graduated from high school at sixteen, to teach or study journalism in college, but instead she had to go to work in the local post office for that dollar a day. That early experience led her to the post office job in Pickstown. The seat behind the post office window was an excellent vantage point for tracking the crosscurrents of the community, for small and large insights into human behavior, and for exchanging small-change gossip with the patrons. My mother was an alert editor. When she came home at the end of the day, she would report to us some astute observation or overheard comment that had a larger lesson. Gordon Larsen was a heating and plumbing maintenance man, a jolly jokester popular with everyone. But the morning after one particularly raucous Halloween, he complained to my mother about the behavior of some teenagers the night before. Mother, trying to make light of it, said, "Oh, c'mon, Gordon, what were you doing when you were seventeen?" "I was landing on Guadalcanal," he said.

When she repeated this at the dinner table, it

gave all of us new insights into Gordon's life; and the comment stayed with me until I began writing *The Greatest Generation*.

Long before the term "sound bite" had been coined, Mother had an ear for one—as any good journalist is always listening for the telling quote. On the day Stalin died, an East European refugee came to Mother's post office window, commented on the death, and said, "They're stoking it up down below today." That was another line Mother didn't leave at work.

Working in such a central location had other bonuses, of course. After school I could drop by and solicit a quarter for a splurge at the drugstore on the corner. Or if I wanted to advertise my lawn-mowing business on the post office's community bulletin board, Mother could make sure the handwritten sign was front and center. My only disappointment during her years there is that although I religiously studied the Most Wanted posters the FBI distributed through the postal system, not once did any of those fugitives cross my path so I could turn them in.

When we moved to Yankton, Mother tried a number of part-time jobs before landing steady work managing a shoe store just off Main

Street. Again, she was in the flow of gossip, the who's up, who's down scorecard that's the staple of life in any small-town business district. She shared quiet but certain observations about the true character of some of the town's leading citizens, being disdainful of the most hypocritical.

Among my friends she was especially popular because she was always quick to put an extra plate on the table when they showed up around suppertime. One friend, a star athlete from a very poor family, thought of Mother as his surrogate mom. Many years later he told her, "You know, Jean, when I showed up for supper so often, it wasn't by accident." She replied, "Oh, Roger—I knew that at the time. We always had room for you," emphasizing his place in our family rather than his difficult circumstances at home.

Other young men from troubled families who were regulars at our dinner table or frequent overnight guests wrote to Mother as adults to thank her for taking them in as if they were sons, feeding them, doing their laundry, and giving them advice. She was so interested in our lives that when I was in high school and arrived home late, I would often yell upstairs and invite her to join a group of pals in the kitchen. She'd come down in her housecoat, with a ready laugh, put on a pot of coffee, and sit down at the kitchen table to share the latest joke or make observations on everything from teenage fads to world events. The next morning my father would just look at the two of us, a little sleepy from the late-night gabfest, shake his head, and recall a couple of old farmers from his hometown who were nonstop talkers.

Mother was my champion but she kept my ego on a short leash. For both my parents, immodesty was right there with slovenliness. Any hint of it and my father was likely to say, "Okay, bigshot, you've got all the answers." Mother had another way of cooling me off.

If I appeared in our small living room, ready for a night out, dressed in what I thought was a snappy number, and asked her, "How do I look?" she was very likely to answer, "Very nice, dear, but what makes you think anyone is going to be looking at you, anyway?"

When I began to appear on television, my father developed a way of dealing with the family's local fame. One night, a stranger introduced himself at the Elks Club and, when he heard the Brokaw name, wanted to know if

Red was related to that guy on television. Dad replied, "Yeah, I think he's a cousin." It got a big laugh at family gatherings.

A few years ago I returned to Yankton as part of a series featuring NBC News correspondents on what had changed in our hometowns since we left. For me, the most striking change was in the status of women. They were now fully integrated into the community's power structure as politicians, lawyers, physicians, and business owners and managers. The girls' teams in high school athletics were a source of community pride and the achievements of young women in other endeavors were celebrated with the enthusiasm once reserved for boys. It was gratifying to see the change—but also a little embarrassing, because it took so long.

However, as I like to say, God knows how to get even. After growing up in that male-dominated culture, I married Meredith and we've had three daughters. They are the beneficiaries of her strengths and those of their Grandma Jean, my mother, who doesn't hesitate to counsel them on all aspects of their lives, which are so much different from her own.

CHAPTER 10

Race

As the American South began its long, often violent struggle over civil rights for Negroes, we in the northern Great Plains felt far removed. On the issue of race we affected a certain moral superiority—or, in many instances, a benign indifference; we had no big-city ghettoes, and we were very far from the Mason-Dixon Line. The shame of the South was not ours to share, or so it seemed at the time.

Our family didn't actually know many Negroes, but they played a prominent role in our lives. My grandfather introduced me to the idea of becoming a Brooklyn Dodgers fan because Branch Rickey had signed Jackie Robinson as the first black Major League baseball player. My father admired Joe Louis, the heavyweight boxing champion, and Jesse Owens, the great Olympic star.

Joe Louis was so much larger than life that as a second grader I wept between rounds when it seemed he was being beaten by Jersey Joe Walcott in their epic 1947 heavyweight fight at Madison Square Garden. We heard the blow-by-blow over the radio in our Ravinia rooming house. I was stunned and overjoyed when Louis won the decision after the radio description of the beating he had taken.

I was an early and enthusiastic fan of the Harlem Globetrotters, the traveling troupe of gifted black basketball players I had seen in Minneapolis. I knew about their origins under Abe Saperstein, a shrewd and tireless promoter who made them into one of America's favorite sports entertainments. Two of their stars—Goose Tatum and Marques Haynes—were in their day on a par with Julius Erving and Allen Iverson, but they were relegated to putting on shows rather than playing real games. Basketball—at the major collegiate and professional level—remained a mostly white sport well after Major League baseball began integration.

At the end of their careers, Tatum and Haynes came to Yankton to play in our community gym on a cold winter night. I was one of a few hundred fans who turned out, and I was excited at the prospect of seeing two of my idols up close. But about halfway through their dispirited performance, I was saddened to realize that it had come to this for two great athletes: relegated to the backwater simply because of their race. Here they were, two of the best basketball players in America, drawing fewer fans than my high school team would in the same gym on the following Friday night. I can still see their weary expressions as they paused on the way to the bus at the end of the game to sign autographs. Then they were off into the South Dakota night for another performance in another out-of-the-way gym, far from the big cities and the big paychecks they deserved.

My father and grandfather had known their share of hard times and they identified with the struggles of these gifted black men. I was an eager heir to Dad and Grandpa's loyalties; it was the beginning of a lifelong interest in race in all of its complexities.

One Pickstown family from the Deep South did little to hide its contempt for Negroes and their struggle. The mother was a tough-talking woman of strong opinions, and one day as she was driving a group of us back from a ball game, she used the "N" word. I challenged her, saying it was wrong to call people by that name. She shot back that it was none of my business what she called them. I didn't give up the fight, and for a time I thought she was going to stop the car and make me walk home. Instead, she finally sputtered in exasperation, "How would you know about words? You people call creeks 'cricks.' " I was only about eleven at the time, but I felt confident I had won the round although probably not the battle.

The appearance of any actual Negro caused a minor stir, more out of curiosity and ignorance than hostility. Pickstown was on a circuit for traveling shows of all kind, including washed-up wrestlers and boxers who staged desultory bouts in portable rings set up on the baseball diamond.

One year two Negro boxers were part of the road show. One had shown some promise back East but his license had been lifted for some infraction, so he was relegated to stagey tank-town matches against his traveling companion, a gentle giant of a man.

When they arrived in Pickstown they imme-diately went into the boys' locker room at the high school, and there they meant to stay until fight time, several hours later. I was maybe ten or eleven, but bold enough to introduce myself and ask if they needed anything. They wanted a couple of sandwiches and so I raced to the drugstore with their order. One of the high school girls on duty said, "Make them come over here for lunch. I want to see them!" With that I gained some insight into why they preferred the sanctuary of the locker room.

For all of my youthful indignation about the treatment of black people, I was unaware of the depth of discrimination against Indians in my home state—this, though many of my friends were Indians: Sylvan Highrock, Peter Archambeau, Armand Hopkins, Elmer Ashes.

As I've mentioned, Pickstown was surrounded by the Yankton Sioux reservation. While Indians were a conspicuous presence, they occupied a distinct and separate place in our universe. They lived in separate sections of the neighboring towns or in rural enclaves, worshiped in their own churches, and drank in what we called Indian bars. They weren't much represented in the labor force at the dam or on the employee rolls of local merchants.

In school we were taught almost nothing

about the rich Indian cultures just beyond our classrooms, but a great deal about Manifest Destiny and the theme that "might makes right." I did not know until many years later that Sitting Bull, the great Sioux chief, had been a prisoner of the 7th Cavalry just across the river at Fort Randall in the late 1800s. I was only vaguely aware of the massacre at Wounded Knee. Yet when I was in grade school that was recent history, really, less than seventy-five years old.

I didn't know that the Sioux had migrated west to the Great Plains from Minnesota and Wisconsin in the 1700s. Although I had a close, easy relationship with my Indian friends, it was not a very discerning one. I didn't know that many of them spoke their native language, Lakotah or Dakotah, at home. I didn't know that the Indian elders preferred the name "Dakotah," their prairie appellation, to "Sioux," the name left behind by French trappers.

I also assumed that any Indian I met was a Sioux, a misapprehension corrected by my seventh-grade friend Jim Welch. When I made some reference to his Sioux ancestry, he retorted, "I am not Sioux; I am Blackfoot and Gros Ventre." These were Montana tribes.

Jim grew up to be a gifted novelist and poet who has written extensively on Indian themes from his home at the University of Montana in Missoula. We reconnected twenty years after our childhood days when his first novel, *Winter in the Blood,* drew rave reviews. I was White House correspondent for NBC at the time and persuaded the *Today* producers to let me interview Jim on the show. I began by saying, "I thought *I* was going to be the first important novelist from our seventh-grade English class."

Alas, when we were in the seventh grade, I was mostly oblivious to the difficulties Jim and other Indians faced every day. I now know there were indefensible instances of discrimination against Indians, especially around the reservations in the western end of the state, in the fifties and sixties. Bars and restaurants prominently displayed signs reading "Indians Not Welcome." The local jails were filled up with drunk Indians on Saturday nights so on Monday morning they could become cheap municipal labor as they worked off their sentences. Alcohol abuse was and continues to be a serious problem in the South Dakota Indian population, but it wasn't confined to Indians. Saturday night was also a hard-drinking time for white farmers, cowboys, and roughnecks, but the drunk tanks were seldom integrated.

As I subsequently learned from my Southern

friends, there were certain parallels in personal relationships between young whites and blacks, and young Indians and whites. We began to drift apart when we reached adolescence, just about the time of serious dating. Most of my Indian friends from junior high moved to the reservation to attend all-Indian schools, where there were many more Indian girls, or they simply dropped out to find work. A few stayed in touch, but only episodically.

Since my family always welcomed my Indian friends at home, and avoided stereotypes, I grew up believing I was a model white boy among the tribes. Twenty years later, as a young reporter in California, I was in the streets of Watts, the black neighborhood that erupted in the 1965 riots. I had been spending a lot of time covering its physical, political, and psychological recovery. Fred Harris, the Oklahoma senator who was then a candidate for the Democratic presidential nomination, was talking to blacks about unemployment. I talked with his wife, who is half Comanche, about Indians.

"Oh, I know a lot about Indians," I said. "I grew up in South Dakota."

LaDonna Harris is a handsome, soft-spoken

woman who looked at me for a moment and then said quietly, "South Dakota is the Mississippi of the Indian nation."

I started to protest, but I realized that only half of my claim was true. I did grow up in South Dakota. But I did not know a lot about Indians. And so I began to read *Bury My Heart at Wounded Knee,* Dee Brown's bestselling Indian history of the American West. The book's title alludes to the 1890 massacre at Wounded Knee, South Dakota, in which hundreds of defenseless Sioux men, women, and children were killed. It was a painful experience, reading of the terror and brutality freely used by the U.S. Army against Indians in clearing the way for white settlers in the 1800s.

I went back to South Dakota in the summer of 1972 to learn more and to write a magazine article for the *Los Angeles Times.*

Growing up, I was always vaguely aware of the attachment the Sioux had to the Black Hills, but I had not realized that it nearly cost them their existence as a people. In the mid-1800s, Sioux tribes roamed the Dakota Territory, moving with the great buffalo herds, their primary source of meat, clothing, shelter, tools, and weapons. Then white hunters moved in with long-range rifles and began a wholesale slaughter of the buffalo for their rich fur and hides.

Alarmed by the rapidly declining buffalo population and the ever-increasing army of white settlers, Spotted Tail of the Sioux and Red Cloud, chief of the Oglala, signed the Fort Laramie Treaty of 1868. It ceded to the federal government nearly all of eastern Dakota and guaranteed to the Sioux "forevermore" much of the western half of the territory, including the Black Hills.

Later, however, when the Black Hills were discovered to be rich with gold, white prospectors and a supporting cast of merchants, prostitutes, and thieves moved into Indian territory in droves, trampling the Fort Laramie Treaty underfoot.

It was the beginning of the last Indian resistance. With the exceptions of General George Custer's defeat at Little Big Horn, and a few other Sioux victories, Indians were beaten into submission by a combination of cavalry bullets, the elimination of the buffalo, and official deceit. They were driven onto Rosebud, Pine Ridge, Standing Rock, and Cheyenne reservations, which now take up about a fifth of western South Dakota, and the Sioux quickly became a minority in their own land.

Once the Indians had been isolated on reservations, white settlers moved in swiftly and shaped the prairie to their own needs, breaking the soil, putting up fences, building houses and churches. They brought "civilization" to Indian territory, and to my generation it was their arrival that marked the beginning of time in South Dakota.

This heritage left me with a twisted sense of reality. I hunted with Indian boys like Sylvan Highrock and ate the meat of the deer his father had killed and smoked. But if I identified with Cochise, I was actually thinking of the actor Jeff Chandler. I heard not a word, nor read a line in my school textbooks, about Sioux history or culture during my formative years.

"Pioneer families had to fight sickness, terrible winters, and marauding Indians," we were taught. Also, "It was necessary for the white hunters to kill the buffalo to feed the hungry work crews laying the railroad track across the hostile prairie." Also, "Christian missionaries risked their lives to bring religion to the heathen tribes." My Indian friends, Peter Archambeau, Sylvan Highrock, Elmer Ashes, and others, listened stoically to what they privately called (as one of them later confided) this "blue-eyed" version of history.

On the walls of the St. Francis Mission museum on the Pine Ridge reservation, a large piece of deerskin contains the Big Missouri's Winter Count, 1795–1917. It's a diary of sorts; each winter along the Missouri is memorialized by a tiny painting of a major event that year. In 1825, for example, a lot of Sioux drowned in a flood, while in 1850 many Sioux died in a smallpox epidemic.

But of all the tragic history represented on the Winter Count, nothing distressed my museum guide, Ida Killer, so much as the symbol for the winter of 1821. It was a jug—for the year the white man brought whiskey to the Sioux.

Roger Scabby Face didn't think there would be much work the year I met him. He spent nearly every fall in Nebraska working on the harvest circuit. But as Scabby Face looked across the scorched prairie, he knew that it was too dry for most crops. So he would probably spend the fall as he had spent the summer—sitting outside his log and mud hut along Highway 18.

There are a half-dozen other hovels scattered across the bare hillside that is identified on the map as the town of Oglala. The only shade was beneath a pine log frame structure covered with pine boughs. Our talk was going well until I asked the name of the pine bough structure under which we were sitting. Madeline Runs Above smiled tightly and answered. "It's an Indian Cooler."

Scabby Face laughed and added, "Sometimes we call it shade."

I immediately recognized my status: dumb white intruder anxious to identify with local color. (Later I learned that in Sioux such a structure is called a *wapakia*.)

At high school in Yankton, I was surrounded by Indian symbolism; Yankton, after all, was named after a Sioux tribe. Our homecoming ceremonies took their name from a vanishing tribe, the Arickara. Cheerleaders stirred up the faithful with a kind of war dance and a chant: "Bucks are on the warpath / Bucks are on the warpath / Get 'em, Bucks / Get 'em"—all that for teams that included such decidedly non-Indian names as Pulkrabek, Pokorney, Kuchta, Soulek, and Cwach.

Princess Struck by the Ree, supposedly a daughter of the great chief of the Yankton tribes, was the mythical mascot of our high school yearbook. Frankly, I always thought Chief Struck by the Ree to be as mythical as the yearbook princess, and so did everyone else I knew. In fact, he was a great chief, a truly historic figure.

Made a U.S. citizen as an infant by Lewis and Clark, Struck by the Ree later fought off dissidents within his tribe to honor the Fort Laramie Treaty. On my 1972 trip, quite by accident, I found his grave—marked by an impressive primitive likeness of the chief—in a small cemetery well off the gravel road that leads to Greenwood, along the Missouri River north of Yankton.

Here lies Padani Apapi
Struck by the Ree

*He was in his day
the most faithful friend
of the white man in
the Sioux nation*

But Struck by the Ree is still a forgotten man in white South Dakota, even among lifelong residents.

When white South Dakota does recognize its Sioux heritage, it usually does so for commercial reasons. Tourism is big business, and travelers are welcomed by colorful brochures that feature Sioux in ceremonial dress. As you drive west across South Dakota on Interstate 90, which acts as a funnel into the Black Hills, signs pop up from the prairie and shout out the coming attractions:

"None Mean—Real Keen. See the prairie dogs. Ranch store."

"Visit the world famous Reptile Gardens in Rapid City."

Tourists driving through the Black Hills see no evidence that this once was sacred land to the Sioux—quite the contrary. A great block of it has been set aside to honor the enemy:

Custer State Park. (Custer did pretty well for a loser. He also has a town named after him. Nothing of official consequence is named after a Sioux hero in South Dakota.)

On the reservations, meanwhile, there has been a revival of authentic Sioux ceremonies for the Indians themselves. A crudely lettered flyer advertised an upcoming sweat lodge ceremony—an ancient Sioux practice of atoning for sin by praying in a hand-fashioned steam bath.

Attention!
Sweat Lodge Ceremony
At
Elijah Blackthunder's
Thursday, July 29
5:30 PM
No women allowed with their period!!
No Drunks!!

Not all Indians, of course, live on reservations. Many have moved to mostly white towns where they settled in poor, all-Indian neighborhoods. In Winner, a contemporary western town on the edge of the Rosebud reservation, a pleasant restaurant cashier was trying to help me locate an address. Suddenly she looked up and said, "That's Indian Town. You want to go there?"

It's not hard to find Indian Town in Winner. The pavement ends at the edge of several blocks of rundown houses and shacks serving as homes. I was looking for Sylvan Highrock, a Yankton Sioux, my friend who had been the Jim Thorpe of the Fort Randall area during my grade school days.

Highrock had been a superb athlete, handsome, strong enough to play high school varsity football at the age of fourteen. In those days he lived with his parents, two sisters, and a brother in a cabin near the Missouri. His father trapped beaver, mink, and muskrat in the winter and worked as a laborer on the dam in the summer, until rising waters forced the family to move to Winner. Shortly before they moved, Sylvan, who had just finished the seventh grade, managed to land a three-month job as a jackhammer operator in the huge intake tunnels of the dam.

As I was getting out of my car, Highrock jumped down off the porch at the side of his narrow frame house, laughing and shouting. "I got your letter," he yelled. "I got your letter."

He said, "Do you remember the time I hit two home runs and got two free movie tickets?"

We went through the "How are you? It's been a long time" routine, each sizing up the other. He laughed again and pointed out that I was now taller. I wanted to say, "You look great," but I couldn't. His once handsome face was disfigured by a severe case of acne. His teeth were in bad shape. I soon realized, too, that he was practically stone deaf. He explained that he had suffered irreversible damage to his ears after working a double shift on the jackhammer that final summer on the dam.

I asked, loudly, if he received any disability compensation. "No," he said, "something happened with paperwork. I never got it." After leaving Fort Randall, he said, he had enrolled in Winner schools, but soon dropped out because he couldn't hear the teachers.

It was a difficult conversation. I had to shout my questions and answers, some of them across twenty years and two worlds.

"You've got a good job?" he asked.

"Yes, in television in California. And you?"

"I work on the garbage truck for the city. It's a good job. I used to work in a body shop fixing cars. The owner sent me to Springfield [a trade school] to learn. Then he sold the shop and the new owner didn't like me."

As we parted, he turned and ran across the parking lot with that familiar, fluid gait, and for an instant I imagined that he was running out onto a football field again, and all would be well. Then he swung easily onto the back of the garbage truck, smiled and waved, and looked straight ahead as the big truck struggled around the corner.

My other friend in Winner was Bob Daughters, one of the white community's leading citizens. We'd known each other since he was student body president at the University of South Dakota during one of my undergraduate years. Daughters went off to Denver for a while, worked for a computer company, married an airline stewardess, and then accepted his brother's invitation to come back to Winner and go into the family livestock business.

During my visit, Daughters was a cheerful host. He was also candid: "I won't hire Indians anymore. We just used 'em for part-time work and we had to pay 'em every night. Even then most would not show up the next day. We don't mind Indians going to the Winner school, but they got the best facility in south central South Dakota out there on the reservation. Why don't they use that? If they started paying their own way, they wouldn't be so demanding. In some of those counties two white men are paying all the taxes.

"You going out to Wounded Knee? They only mow the grass around the place for tourists. Anyway, that happened a long time ago. We can't be responsible for that."

The year was 1890. Shortly after Christmas, cavalry units caught up with Chief Big Foot and a small, tattered band of Minneconjou Sioux at a creek called Wounded Knee on the Pine Ridge reservation. Big Foot was returning to the reservation after leaving it for a few days to defy Army orders against practicing the Ghost Dance, a Sioux religious ceremony in which Indians had visions of their invulnerability.

The defenseless Indians were cut down by the withering fire. No one is sure how many were killed—at least 150, perhaps as many as 350.

When I visted in 1972, Wounded Knee had changed only a little since 1890. There was a small trading post and museum for the few tourists who were curious enough to leave the main highway and drive to the country cross-roads identified on Department of Highway maps as "Wounded Knee Battlefield."

In 1973, Wounded Knee became the site of a standoff between activists from AIM, the American Indian Movement, federal and state authorities, and factions of the Oglala tribe on the Pine Ridge Reservation. Two FBI agents were shot and killed, and one of the activists, Leonard Peltier, is now serving a life sentence in Leavenworth Federal Prison.

When I toured Wounded Knee, behind the museum, where many of Big Foot's followers were trapped that day eighty-one years before, Wounded Knee Creek was dry, filled with waist-high weeds and the litter of a recent powwow on nearby dancing grounds. I walked along the creek bed, pushing through the weeds, and looked for a long time toward the hill where the guns had been positioned.

There was a church there, and a small grave-yard. The grass was mowed around a long, nar-row plot outlined in concrete. This is the mass grave of the Wounded Knee victims. A six-foot-high stone marker contains some of their names—Chief Big Foot, High Hawk, Black

Coyote, Young Afraid of Bear, and even White America—along with a simple inscription:

*Many innocent women and children
who knew no wrong died here*

In the museum, I asked an Iowa woman, touring with her children, if she understood what happened here, at Wounded Knee. She hesitated for a moment, and then said, uncertainly, "There was an awful lot of Indians killed."

That trip reawakened my interest in South Dakota's native population, although I harbored no dreamy and romantic images of the modern Sioux. The tribes suffer from too much poverty and too much racism, but they also carry the self-inflicted wounds of alcoholism and drug abuse. Their struggle to exist in a culture alien to them is at once heartbreaking and frustrating. There has been real, measurable economic progress on several of the reservations and in the relations between whites and Indians in South Dakota, but there is far to go.

Bob Daughters, my friend in Winner, stayed in touch as I moved from California to Washington, D.C., and to New York. Periodically, he'd send me a pair of cowboy boots because, as he put it, "I hate to think of you in New York without a pair of boots." After he died of cancer in his thirties, his widow found a handwritten note among his personal papers, instructing her to send me all of his unopened boxes of cowboy boots. A dozen pair arrived at our apartment in New York.

I loved the sentiment from my cowboy-tough friend, but well before his death I was even more impressed that he had been quietly keeping track of Sylvan Highrock. One day Bob called to say that Sylvan—not yet forty—had died of cirrhosis of the liver. I arranged to have a headstone engraved and placed at his burial site on the Rosebud reservation.

When I was a child there was so much I didn't understand about the complexity of the Indian-white relationship in my home state. As an adult, I came to realize that the whites who settled the Dakota Territory represented strong, well-defined cultures centered on community, church, education, and work. Many of them couldn't understand why the Indians didn't just automatically assimilate and adopt their way of life; they failed to appreciate that the Dakotah culture had its own rhythms and rituals.

After I left South Dakota there was a growing

consciousness on both sides of the racial divide about the need to find common ground, but that search remains, at best, a work in progress.

In the summer of 2001 I returned to what remains of Pickstown to write an article for *National Geographic.* I found my old friend Armand Hopkins, a Yankton Sioux who was a grade-school classmate. He was spending most of his evenings watching the gamblers at the Fort Randall Casino the Yankton tribe operates on a hilltop overlooking the dam.

Armand remembered the names of most of our sixth-grade classmates and our teachers. He said his brief years in Pickstown were the best of his young life, and laughed when I recalled skipping school to go fishing near his father's farm. But the names of other friends produced a depressing litany.

"Where's Peter Archambeau?"

"Dead," Armand said.

"Elmer Ashes?"

"Dead, they're all dead."

They're dead and I am alive and flourishing, not just because we had different ambitions and skills. It is not lost on me that all of my good fortune in life and my career would have been neutralized at the outset if my skin had been a few shades darker. I would not have gotten that first job in Omaha or the second one in Atlanta two and a half years later. There were no people of color working in the newsrooms of either city in the early and mid-1960s. In the network newsrooms, where the battle for civil rights was the defining issue of the early days of Huntley-Brinkley and Walter Cronkite, racial diversity was at best a notion.

When America first began to seriously confront racial inequalities in the sixties, mobilized by the courage and eloquence of Dr. Martin Luther King, Jr., and his equally brave and determined followers, I naively believed we would cure the cancerous effects of racism in my lifetime. I now know that is not true. Race remains a central issue in the evolution of our political, economic, and cultural environment. It continues to haunt me personally; I am grateful that my formative years in the mostly white environment of the upper Midwest sharpened my sensibilities about the inequities and the complexities of race for the rest of my life.

CHAPTER 11

Failure Is an Option

IF I WERE EQUIPPED WITH ONE OF THOSE black boxes that are so useful in determining what went wrong in an airplane crash, I might be able to cite a moment or an incident when my life, my personal flight plan, suddenly veered off course and careened along a dangerous trajectory for more than two years. Sometime in my senior year in high school, when I turned eighteen, I began a steady descent into a pattern of self-deception, conceit, and irresponsibility. Now, more than forty years later, I am persuaded it was an early case of hubris brought on by an inability to place schoolboy achievement and flattery in a proper perspective. In short, admonitions from my father aside, I thought I was hot stuff and entitled to a life solely on my terms.

By the second semester of my senior year in high school I was riding high: a Harvard alum was encouraging me to apply for admission; I was a starting guard on the varsity basketball team and president of the student council; I had been elected governor of Boys State the preceding spring; the real governor of South Dakota, Joe Foss, often summoned me to the state capital to preside over events for teenagers; I was spending more weekends on the fraternity party circuit at the nearby University of South Dakota; and I was picking up medals and ribbons as a member of the high school forensics club.

Nonetheless, there were warning signs that the Brokaw orbit was about to develop some ominous irregularities. A telling moment occurred when I was expected to participate in an extemporaneous drill during a forensics class. The teacher that day was a no-nonsense substitute, Mrs. Holmes, a formidable woman who, given my reputation, probably expected a stellar performance when I arose to speak on the assigned subject. The fact is, I had not prepared at all and so I winged it, in full bloviating fashion. When I sat down there was an awkward silence until Mrs. Holmes flatly declared, "Brokaw, you're a fraud."

The other students, earnest and dedicated

*In 1957, the year I was Boys State
governor—outside our home
at 1515 Mulberry.*

debaters, burst into appreciative laughter, delighted that this flashy intruder from the jock set had been nailed. As for me, I knew I had been justly busted, but I laughed it off. In retrospect, it took an outsider to say, in effect, "The boy has no clothes."

Alas, it didn't alter my course. By spring I was on a tear of self-indulgence, coasting through the final weeks of class and spending more time with hard-drinking older friends at the University of South Dakota. I had the lead in the all-school play, the final production of the term, but I had failed to learn all my lines, so the director called an extraordinary Saturday-night rehearsal before the Tuesday opening just for my benefit.

I was competing in a track meet that day and failed to qualify for the state competition. This put me in a what-the-hell mood, so I skipped the rehearsal and headed for the Beta Theta Pi fraternity house twenty-five miles away. Sometime after midnight I arrived home in a wobbly condition. My father was waiting for me in the front room. He had fielded several calls that evening, saying I was expected at the rehearsal. He had assured the callers I would be there, because in his mind there were few greater

Student Council

As student council president, 1958,
I'm checking in with high school principal
Don R. Snowden, a favorite.

faults than not living up to your responsibilities and expectations.

He demanded an explanation. When I tried to brush him off, I suddenly found myself on the staircase landing. Dad had simply grabbed me with one hand and pitched me there. I weighed 180 pounds at the time and I was in peak condition, but I was not interested in a further test of Red Brokaw's fury, so I scrambled off to bed, promising as I went that I would, as Dad insisted, call everyone the next day and apologize.

I did that, but I was expelled from the play, as I should have been. There were some awkward moments in the hallways when I encountered the other cast members, and especially the student director. She was someone I admired, but I had never been able to win her confidence. She didn't completely trust my style, finding it too cute by half. Her name was Meredith Auld. Once again, the girl from the trombone case had reason to wonder about my reliability.

After graduation I headed for the University of Iowa, a Big Ten school with a reputation for academic excellence and a powerhouse football team. One of my high school classmates, the estimable quarterback Bill Whisler, was

Meredith Auld in 1958.
She was always attentive in
class—and wary of my style.

going there on a full football scholarship, and I was attracted to its bucolic setting along the Iowa River.

I had seen the university briefly in the spring of my senior year in high school. My father and I had made the long drive from Yankton because I had been encouraged to apply in person for a food services job at the dorm where I would be staying. I needed the extra money to help pay the out-of-state tuition.

So Dad and I left Yankton around three in the morning for a nine A.M. appointment. He stayed in the car as I went in for what turned out to be a perfunctory dismissal of my chances by a stern middle-aged woman with a tightly wound personality and a hairdo to match. She'd responded to my application only as a courtesy, she said; all the jobs had been filled.

When I reported this to Red, who was napping in the car after the long drive, I had to practically physically restrain him from charging into her office to raise hell about our treatment. Since all campus environments were new to him and this one was unknown to me, we made a quick tour and then bolted for relatives in the northern part of the state to spend the night.

We were little more prepared when Mother

Meredith as Miss South Dakota, 1959.

and Dad dropped me off for the fall term. The University of Iowa was one of the smaller Big Ten schools, but its students outnumbered the population of Yankton, so I was suddenly a very small fish in a much larger pond. More-over, many of the students were from Chicago or its affluent suburbs and they carried with them a self-assurance I had only rarely encoun-tered in South Dakota.

Most of all, I really didn't quite know what to expect in college. My high school had no college counselors, no one in my family had attended college, and my only experience on a campus had been at drunken fraternity parties or the occasional speech tournament. I guess I thought it was an extension of high school in a grander setting. Unfortunately, that's how I treated it. My one year at Iowa was at once memorable and embarrassing.

Memorable, because I wasn't so dim that I failed to appreciate the strengths of a great uni-versity and what it means to the state it serves. I still remember encounters with bright young professors from the department of history; writers in the famed Writers Workshop; James Van Allen, the celebrated astrophysicist; and wonkish graduate students deep in the stacks of the library late at night. I was also voted one of the outstanding freshmen ROTC cadets and in the spring of my freshman year I was selected to emcee the Mother's Day festivities on campus, a rare honor for a freshman.

Those were episodic highlights, however, and not representative of how I spent most of my time. Instead of hitting the books with dedication, I cruised the student union, bedazzled by the rich population of fetching coeds, especially those from the moneyed suburbs of north Chicago. I also tucked myself into a corner of a gathering place for the small population of black students, to watch them dance and listen to the coolest music on campus. I drank beer and played pool and seldom studied for an exam until the night before, if then. I sold blood at the student infirmary to finance dinner dates and I never missed a football or basketball game. I joined a fraternity and failed to make the grades required for full membership.

I returned to Yankton and a summer job at KYNT with my friend Chuck Ruhr, who had just graduated from the University of South Dakota. Chuck was headed to Minneapolis and what turned out to be a very successful career in advertising, but first we decided to turn the summer into a long party of boat rides on the lake, road trips to the Black Hills and an Iowa resort, and late nights at Yankton's several drinking establishments. For Chuck, it was a diversion before pursuing his well-organized ambitions. For me, it was business as usual.

At the beginning of my sophomore year I decided to retreat to the University of South Dakota to get my act together. Instead, I continued the same pattern of behavior, compounding it by making late-night, expensive phone calls back to the coeds I'd left behind at the University of Iowa. Simultaneously, I was unsuccessfully pursuing Meredith Auld, my high school classmate, the one who had always resisted my charms. Even if she had not been the reigning Miss South Dakota she would have been atop anyone's list: she was bright, beautiful, popular, and mature beyond her nineteen years.

We had a cordial dating relationship, but it was clear she was not interested in anything long-term with me. I was not accustomed to rejection and I was too self-absorbed to engage in any realistic analysis of why she might feel that way. If I had taken just a small step outside my behavior and examined it from her perspective, it would have been clear. I didn't belong to a fraternity, which left me free to attend the parties of all of them. My weight had ballooned up to a portly two hundred pounds as a result of a steady diet of beer and pizza. I was a serial flirt. In fact, if I had pursued my studies with just half the fervor I dedicated to girls and good times, I would have been Phi Beta Kappa.

Too many mornings, I awoke with a blinding hangover, having slept through one class and unprepared for the next. I'd look into the mirror and resolve to straighten out immediately. The resolve would last until the next invitation to make a road trip to some out-of-town party or to celebrate the first blizzard of the season with a long night of beer-drinking games at the Varsity, the local student pub.

I masked my errant ways to some extent by working hard at two radio stations, but I lost one of those those jobs when I left in the middle of a shift to attend a friend's wedding *and* the reception. A major storm warning had blown up while I was away from the news desk and the lone announcer on duty was not happy when I returned after an afternoon of drinking champagne.

Midway through my second semester as a sophomore, I was invited to dinner at the home of W. O. "Bill" Farber, the University of South Dakota's legendary political science professor and chairman of the department, where I was supposed to be one of his star students. He'd been on campus since the mid-thirties and he was celebrated as a mentor to many of the state's governors, U.S. senators, congressmen, and other high-ranking public servants. He also had an enviable record as a producer of Rhodes Scholars from the small land-grant university.

After an agreeable dinner, Bill turned to me and cheerfully began a conversation that saved my life. He said, "Tom, I've been thinking about you." "You have?" I was secretly delighted at being on Farber's agenda. But then he went on. "Yes," he said, "I think you should drop out of school. Get all of this wine, women, and song out of your system and come back when you'll do yourself some good, your parents, and this school." I can still see him sitting in his Barcalounger as he stunned me, his hands crossed on his ample midsection, a pleasant but determined expression on his face.

I had mixed feelings. I hated being exposed as a slacker, but I rather relished the encouragement to raise hell to the point of exhaustion. Besides, I always believed this was just a passing phase and I could turn it around anytime I wanted. (Later I saw the same deepseated denial while reporting on drug addicts, drunks, and various others who had somehow lost control of their lives.)

I think that part of the denial actually lay in my strong interest in politics. I confused real personal achievement with my keen interest in the historic race that had developed for the Democratic and Republican presidential nominations in 1960. Richard Nixon, John Kennedy, and Lyndon Johnson were the first of their generation to have a clear chance at the White House. My parents were never going to vote for Nixon, and LBJ seemed too Texas for them. Still, they were also suspicious of JFK for his Eastern ways, his rich father, and his Catholicism. They wondered if he could ever identify with their problems, and I think they were suspicious of the Kennedy sense of entitlement. Most of South Dakota could identify with Nixon and Johnson; they were not unlike the men I had known growing up. They were from poor families and they had worked hard to get to their positions of power without the built-in advantage of privileged birth. But to me, both looked as if they were always trying too hard. Their wardrobes were ordinary, and their friends matched their wardrobes.

But Kennedy—my God, he was so dashing with all those handsome siblings and a wife who was more elegant than European royalty. Now we know there was much the Kennedys kept from us, but in 1960 JFK was a transformational candidate. And as someone who was always curious about life beyond my own well-defined cosmos, I thought he would take us to new heights. I thought the John F. Kennedy élan would define the rest of my life. It lasted less than three years.

During the summer of 1960, when the political process was in full throttle, I was working for a CBS affiliate in Rapid City, South Dakota, covering the local races and George McGovern's unsuccessful first run for the U.S. Senate. I was learning the rudiments of broadcast journalism by day and I even met Mike Wallace when he stopped by the newsroom. But by night I was up to my old tricks of girls, beer, and partying. Rapid City is the gateway to the Black Hills, a popular summer resort area, so there was no shortage of festive times, especially when the Days of '76 rolled around.

They were staged in the historic town of Deadwood to commemorate the era of Wild Bill Hickok and Calamity Jane.

During the Days of '76, college students from several states converged for three days of bacchanal. I was a leader of the pack. Late one night, after the bars had closed, a friend and I decided to put on a show in an unlikely setting: an all-night Laundromat. I crawled into one of the big tumble dryers, my friend closed the door just enough to activate the cycle, and I rode the dryer for several rotations, emerging to the cheers of the crowd. As the local police tried to make their way through the throng, my friend and I slipped into the bathroom and out the rear window.

I arrived home at the end of the summer with a cowboy hat and fifty cents in my pocket. Despite my meager resources, I told my parents I would make my way in the world by dropping out of college for a time. My father took all this in and immediately lined up a job for me digging post holes by hand for the foundation of a new house for his boss. He also—literally—physically barred my way when I announced I was heading to California to find work. Red knew that whatever my chances of recovering equilibrium, California wasn't the answer.

I made a couple of trips back to the South Dakota campus and unsuccessfully tried to arrange a date with Meredith. She answered by mail with a letter that was more than a Dear John. It was a notice that I was not to call again. It was clear, she said, that I was headed nowhere fast; why would she waste her time with someone so irresponsible?

I was stunned and immediately took the letter to our mutual friend Bob Legvold, my running mate from Boys State, who was already married and preparing for his career in Russian studies. I can still remember him pausing on the campus to read what I thrust into his hands. He finished it, folded it, handed it back to me, and said in his cool, analytical way, "I think she's right."

It was a blow that coming from the two of them should have prompted me to reform on the spot. Instead, I hitchhiked to a small town in Minnesota, where I was hired as a nighttime disc jockey at a radio station. I rented a room and walked two miles to the station for five days before I was fired for insubordination brought on by my own cocky attitude and the station owner's small-minded ways.

My one enduring memory from that week is that a crewcut young candidate for attorney general of Minnesota came by the station as part of a campaign tour. I recognized him as a rising star in state politics and urged the news director to interview him but, typically, the tape recorder didn't work. When I asked him about it many years later, the politician claimed he remembered the moment. His name was Walter "Fritz" Mondale; he became a U.S. senator, vice president of the United States, and, in 1984, the Democratic presidential candidate.

At the end of my week in Minnesota I was on the road again, hitchhiking back to South Dakota and my parents' home. There, on election night in 1960, a small bulb began to burn through my consciousness. I stayed up all night, watching the NBC News team led by Chet Huntley and David Brinkley as the returns seesawed back and forth between Nixon and Kennedy. Finally, well after dawn, NBC News projected Kennedy the winner. I was bedazzled by the historic moment and the informed byplay among the correspondents—John Chancellor, Sander Vanocur, Edwin Newman, and the others. Although it was not a "Eureka!" experience, I began to see the outlines of a career.

Of course, I still had a good deal of reform-ing ahead. As usual, Mother was a key player. One morning when I came down for breakfast she was watching the local news from KTIV, the NBC affiliate in Sioux City. The news-caster was less than amateurish, and Mother said matter-of-factly: "You could do better than that. Why don't you apply for his job? Your father and I will drive you to Sioux City." I made an appointment with the station personnel director, Don Stone, and Mother and Dad deposited me at the station.

He hired me as a staff announcer, part-time weatherman, and substitute newscaster for $75 a week. I rented a room; since I didn't have a car, I walked to work and depended on the kindness of strangers and friends to get around.

Quickly, I adapted to my new environment. I liked the young production crew, many of them part-time students like me, and the pro-fessional full-timers, including an ambitious young graduate of the Medill School of Jour-nalism at Northwestern. His name was David Schoumacher, and this was his first job after fulfilling an Air Force obligation. He brought a serious, professional attitude to his duties, and I became something of a protégé.

Schoumacher had ambition and the training to pursue it. Others at the station were stuck in low-paying dead-end jobs because they didn't have an education; it didn't take me long to decide which course had the most promise. I discovered a car pool of students commuting to the University of South Dakota forty miles away, and I made arrangements to join it.

I went back to Dr. Farber and begged to be readmitted. He said, "Okay, but on my terms." He filled out a schedule that had me in class between eight A.M. and noon and then back into the car to commute to my room and job in Sioux City. I worked until eleven most nights and arose at six to commute back to class.

Between paying room and board and most of my college costs, I had very little left over, so I took a weekend job at a radio station and slowly began to rebuild my reputation for reliability. At the television station I befriended the guest chefs for a cooking show called *Man in the Kitchen* and persuaded them to make extra portions of my favorite meals, which I then stretched over a couple of days.

Toward the end of my first semester back on campus, I was in the library when Meredith approached. It was a moment I had been dreading, because I was still embarrassed by her assessment of me in the fall. She asked me to take her to coffee because there was something she wanted to get off her mind.

When we settled in a favorite campus gathering place, she said something to the effect of "I had no right to send you that letter. It wasn't my place to judge you. I'm sorry." I quickly assured her she had done the right thing, even though it hurt at the time. I had it coming, I said. Then I inquired about her boyfriend. When she said they had broken up, I tried to sound casually sympathetic, but my true feeling was "Thank you, Lord." Just as casually, I asked her if she wanted to catch a movie on the weekend. When she said yes, my turnaround moved to much higher ground.

I continued to commute between classes and work while making a reentry into campus life. Meredith and I were soon seeing each other full-time and I was trying to become a responsible student citizen again, getting respectable if not prizewinning grades, working two broadcasting jobs, writing a column for the student newspaper, and never missing *The Huntley-Brinkley Report,* with its news of the space race, the civil rights movement, Castro's defiant full embrace of Communism, the glamorous antics of John F. Kennedy's inner circle, and reports of American military advisers being sent to a little country called Vietnam.

In our senior year, Meredith suggested something I was too intimidated to mention: marriage. Many of our friends were being married right after graduation, and by this time Meredith and I were inseparable and deeply in love. She was just twenty and I was twenty-one. That now seems impossibly young, but it was not unusual in the early sixties to get married at that age. We began to plan the ceremony around my expected basic training in some branch of the military.

For young men, military service was mandatory and I was eager to join the Navy officer training program. I had a romantic notion of running PT boats just like JFK had. America was not at war, so there was no urgency, but I wanted to get my obligation out of the way and earn officer's pay while doing it. It was stunning, then, when the Navy rejected me as an officer candidate solely because I had flat feet. The recruiter was equally stunned and suggested I write my congressman to get a waiver.

I said I'd rather first get a reading from the

Army induction doctors since the draft was my next concern. The Army also rejected me on the basis of my flat feet, even though I had been an athlete and an active outdoorsman. It was, I suppose, a sign of the peaceful times: three years later, as Vietnam was beginning to heat up, my brother Bill, with feet as flat as mine, was in uniform shortly after his induction physical.

I was able to get a job in the newsroom of KMTV, the NBC affiliate in Omaha. The news director, Mark Gautier, was impressed with my knowledge of American politics and offered me $90 a week to start as a basic reporter. I held out for $100, explaining that I was about to marry the daughter of a physician and I needed to make a stronger impression. Mark reluctantly agreed. (Twenty years later, when I signed a multimillion-dollar contract with NBC, Mark wrote to say, "They should have let me negotiate your contract, Tom. I got you for a lot less.")

Meredith's father, Merritt Auld, was, I realize in retrospect, a man of generous faith in his daughter's judgment. A highly respected physician, a leading citizen in our community, and a decorated World War II veteran, he had reason to expect his firstborn would marry someone much more promising than me. But with the strong endorsement of Meredith's equally impressive mother, Vivian, he was unequivocally supportive and that was a huge boost to my self-esteem. As for my mother and dad, Jean and Red, they were elated that I was not only back on track but also about to bring them a daughter of their dreams. Life was beginning to look up for their son, who had so worried and puzzled them.

Meredith and I were married on August 17, 1962, in Yankton. On that same day, John Kennedy made his only trip to South Dakota as president, so we shared newspaper space if not status. In fact, our position in life was based primarily on promise; we had little more than a trunkful of wedding gifts, innocent young love, and a spirit of adventure . . . up to a point.

We honeymooned one night at the Flamingo Motel in South Sioux City, then headed south on the interstate to begin our new lives in Omaha, a city with which we were mostly unfamiliar. Arriving on the outskirts around dusk, we decided to stay in the smaller city of Council Bluffs, Iowa, across the river, because we were worried about getting lost in Omaha after dark.

The next day we drove into Omaha and our new life together, two children of the fifties and the firstborn in families that shared values and a culture. We were innocents in a world about to undergo a radical transformation. All the navigational charts of our childhood would be called into question, if not thrown into disrepute. Without compromising our instinct for new experiences, we managed to keep our bearings because of the way and the place in which we had been raised. Since that muggy night in August 1962, we've come to many more bridges into the unknown and we've learned that crossing them is almost always more rewarding than staying on the familiar side of the river.

CHAPTER 12

Reflections

ALL REGIONS AND ALL ERAS INFLUENCE those who come of age in them. I've often joked that if I had grown up in California in the fifties, I'd be a blond six-foot-two surfer and rock star. I have a great affinity with my friends from the South who were raised in a storytelling culture, from the blues to folktales. New Yorkers my age recall fondly the friendlier rhythms of city life and the richness of a young life when public schools were superior, culture was always at hand, and prices for everything from Dodgers, Yankees, and Giants games to concert tickets and dinners out were affordable. As for me, I will always be a child of the Great Plains and a direct descendant of those who bent their backs against the soil and hard times and held true to their bearings.

However, my life has also been richer for the mix of experiences that come with living in the South, the West, and the East after my Great Plains childhood. As an adult, and from a distance, I have also come to understand that had I stayed in the Midwest, I likely would have struggled with some of the enduring traits of the region. When I read *Main Street,* Sinclair Lewis's novel of Gopher Prairie, Minnesota, his withering description of the boorish and small-minded culture that can suffocate un-conventional attitudes and free spirits was uncomfortably close to a truth I was reluctant to fully embrace. When my friends who stayed in South Dakota ask how I can possibly deal with all of the people and the quick-step pace of city life, I hedge, answering that it's a struggle but, in fact, I am stimulated by all of the life forms in a city and the choices that come with living there.

I always tried to get the best out of my surroundings, including the lessons that come with the conventions and the excesses, the stereotypes and the expectations. Saul Bellow has written, "The commonest teaching of the civilized world in our time can be stated simply: 'Tell me where you come from and I will tell you what you are.' " Bellow was adamant

The happy beginning of a long journey.
Our wedding day, August 17, 1962.
Left to right: Merritt and Vivian Auld,
Meredith, me, Mother and Dad.

about the stereotyping that comes with being Chicago born and raised, commenting, "I couldn't say why I would not allow myself to become a product of an environment. But gainfulness, utility, prudence, business had no hold on me."

In retracing the contours of my life for this book, I have been trying to pay tribute to what I carried out of the heartland that still serves me well. This personal odyssey began just before the attacks on America of September 11, 2001. The long days and nights that followed were the most challenging in my career. I later said it took everything I had learned personally and professionally to get through them.

At the same time Meredith and I were preparing to mark our fortieth wedding anniversary with a family reunion and a celebration of our good fortune as personified by our daughters, Jennifer, Andrea, and Sarah, our son-in-law, Allen, and our granddaughters, Claire Vivian and Meredith Bryant. We celebrated in Yankton in the summer of 2002 with three days of reminiscing and parties with two hundred friends and family members.

So this return to the memories and lessons of an earlier life has been comforting and yet sometimes bewildering. It reminded me again of the forces that shaped me and how powerful and protective they were.

My family and community, however frustrated they may have been with my excesses or failings, never abandoned me. From them I learned to take the long view, especially during a crisis. As someone who works in the bright lights of a public medium, it is important that I came of age surrounded by those for whom the intrinsic reward of labor is a job well done, no matter whether many or a few people may have witnessed the result.

It is also bewildering because when I set out from that time and place I had no full realization of the distances involved, however you measure them. South Dakota is a long way from where and how I live now. I am reminded of that when, often late at night, I am awakened by my lifelong nocturnal restlessness and begin an aimless prowl through our spacious New York apartment. Wandering from the kitchen through the dining room to the large and comfortable living room with the library off to the side, I ponder my good fortune and long run of luck and wonder, "How did this happen? How did I get from *there* to *here*?"

Our library bay window looks south, across the Manhattan skyline. On the morning of September 11, 2001, I could see great black clouds of smoke rising into the late-summer sky shortly after the first airliner hit the World Trade Center. I was dressing hurriedly, having been summoned by my office to cover what we initially thought was a small plane accident.

It was not, of course. For the next two weeks I would return home late at night and stare numbly south to a skyline now framed by the sulfurous glow rising from lower Manhattan, where powerful work lights illuminated the site of the attack. The attack and all of its consequences had taken over my professional life and profoundly affected my personal compass. After residing in New York for more than a quarter of a century, and becoming deeply involved in the longitude and latitude of city life, I had begun to take my attachment to the city for granted. After September 11, I could feel a visceral bonding with my adopted home.

The events of September 11 were also a reminder of the innocence of my childhood in South Dakota in the forties and fifties. I have taken to saying that when I was a young man and thinking I might want to become a journalist, I used to worry that all of the big events had already happened. When John F. Kennedy was assassinated during my first year in a news-room, my naiveté was shattered, and for the next forty years I have been a traveler on a landscape of great, wrenching change.

The world in which I work and live is a long way from home, but the early bearings I took as a child on the prairie, surrounded by working people and the communities they established, often in difficult circumstances, have been a steadying and reassuring presence. They are familiar markers and sentinels, useful and reli-able even now, forty years after I left the land and the people that launched me.

ABOUT THE AUTHOR

TOM BROKAW is the author of three best-sellers: *The Greatest Generation, The Greatest Generation Speaks,* and *An Album of Memories.* A native of South Dakota, Tom Brokaw graduated from the University of South Dakota with a degree in political science. He began his journalism career in Omaha and Atlanta before joining NBC News in 1966. Brokaw was the White House correspondent for NBC News during Watergate, and from 1976 to 1981 he anchored *Today* on NBC. He has been the sole anchor and managing editor of *NBC Nightly News with Tom Brokaw* since 1983. Brokaw has won every major award in broadcast journalism, including two DuPonts, a Peabody Award, and several Emmys. He lives in New York and Montana.